How *not* to Hire
A Guy Like Me

Lessons Learned from CEOs' Mistakes

Lee N. Katz

Schroder Media

Schroder Media

Published by Schroder Media LLC
P.O. Box 250026
Atlanta, Georgia 30325

Cover and book design: Heidi Rizzi
Production editor: Jan Schroder
Index: Joanne Sprott

ISBN: 978-0-9762288-8-2

Printed and bound in the United States

To my wife, Arlene...

I couldn't get through life
without you.

To Jay Solomon and Eszter Boda....

Your high energy, sense of humor and
dedication, including editing while
traveling around the globe, made this book
possible. I'll be forever grateful for your
love and support throughout this project.

Business leaders' comments
about Lee's book,

How Not to Hire a Guy Like Me

Lee's calming influence and unique problem-solving abilities are his trademarks. His clients appreciate that he rolls up his sleeves and gets the job done. He's respected throughout the industry for his professionalism and successes.

—Jerry Goldress
CEO & Founder
Grisanti, Galef & Goldress, Inc.

Experience is, by far, the best teacher. How many of us, in the course of running our businesses, have uncovered millions of dollars in fraud, been forced to lay off thousands of employees, renegotiated billions of dollars in commercial leases, and been fired at by Uzis and shotguns? Lee Katz has survived all these situations—and lots more—in his thirty-year career as a turnaround specialist. You name it, Lee has done it. Fortunately, Lee has shared his invaluable experiences with us in this extraordinary book. We can learn from the mistakes of others, through the wizardry and humor of Lee Katz.

—Alex Gregory
Chairman of the Board
President and CEO of YKK Corporation of America

Years ago I gave Lee the nickname "Gumby" for his uncanny ability to help business clients get out of the tightest spots with nimbleness and flexibility. Given Lee's schedule, it is hard to imagine when he was able to write a book, but how fortunate that he did find the time to share his insights, practical advice, and characteristic good humor.

—**Ann-Ellen Hornidge Esq.**
Partner
Mintz Levin

I have known Lee Katz for many years. Fortunately, I usually see him at a table when he is doing philanthropic work in the community.

When I co-founded The Home Depot, we were creating a business – actually an industry – that had never existed previously. The potential for making catastrophic mistakes was always just around the corner.

Fortunately, I was blessed with partners and associates who were long on wisdom and good sense, and short on ego and selfishness. We were able to avoid the pitfalls that Lee defines so well.

What you are about to uncover inside this book can help ensure that you, as a leader, also avoid pitfalls. Read it. Learn from it. Benefit from Lee's many years as The Turnaround Authority. That way, the only time you will ever see Lee's face is either on this cover, or smiling across the table at a philanthropic endeavor.

— **Bernie Marcus**
Chairman
The Marcus Foundation

I've known Lee Katz for more than thirty years. He has found a way to do his work with caring and integrity and an unswerving commitment to both doing things right ... and doing the right thing. Lee's book, calling on his experience as the Turnaround Authority™, provides us lessons on staying out of trouble as well as getting out of trouble. Lee teaches us that success is not always permanent…but the same is also true of failure.

—**Harry Maziar**
Retired Chairman Chemical Division, National Service Industries
Executive-in-Residence, Kennesaw State University

Lee demonstrates the ability to identify the root causes of adverse business situations and develop actionable plans for restoring stability and profitability. To benefit from his experiences as a turnaround specialist without suffering the pain of living through the process is the beauty of this book.

— Jess Meyers
Former Chief Financial Officer of Ocean Pacific

Lee Katz covers what they didn't teach you in business school—how to avoid the land mines and what to do if you happen to step on one. The book is filled with outstanding nuggets of wisdom for any business leader.

—Rafael Pastor
Chief Executive Officer
Vistage International, Inc.

Table of Contents

Chapter 3

Be Proactive, Not Reactive   37

Chapter 4

Danger Signs and Dollar Signs:
How to Make Your Banker Your Partner   57

Chapter 5
Fraud: Stop It Before It Starts   73

Chapter 6
The Big Picture   93

Introduction

It was 10:15 in the morning, and I was sitting at a red light in Juarez, Mexico, leagues from the US border. This was the only stoplight for miles in either direction—perhaps the only intersection at all. There were no other cars on the road. As I sat at a standstill awaiting a green light, I saw a motorcycle cop roaring towards me from the opposite direction, with his lights swirling and siren blaring. He went flying past me, made a dramatic U-turn that I watched in my rearview mirror, and pulled his motorcycle right beside me—a car I'd rented a few hours earlier in Texas to drive across the border and make my way to a local factory.

I needed to figure out why the El Paso company that owned this factory in Mexico was in such bad shape. The books indicated that its shrinkage rate was through the roof and that the employee turnover rate at this factory was 17 percent per month. That's a ruinous number when you have 500 employees, especially considering the investment in HR and training. Sitting at the traffic light with this cop hovering over me, though, brought me to the moment and minimized the relevance of shrinkage and turnover rates.

The cop attempted, in less-than-stellar English, to tell me that I'd been speeding in a school zone and that I'd just run a red light. We both looked at the light where I'd been easily sitting for two minutes—perhaps the only light in memory for either of us that day—and then turned back to each other. He stared at me, deadpan. After a few moments of silence he walked around to the back of my car, removed my license plate, and drove off. Seems about right, I thought.

With the cop gone I continued to the factory. I had just been appointed CEO of the company that owned this factory, a company that made, ironically enough, the switches for the signals used in traffic lights—switches like the one that left me stranded at that stoplight awaiting my friendly neighborhood "law" enforcer.

Upon arriving at the factory, I shared what had happened to me with the plant manager, asking him if I should have bribed the cop with $100 to move on and keep my license plate. He said that the cop would have found that amount insulting, and that at this point, if I wanted my license plate back—the only way I was going to get this rental car back across the border—I was going to have to bribe him with $500. As it happens, I carry at least that much with me in cash on any job, and luckily for me, the plant manager knew the cop. He assured me that he'd take the fine officer the $500 to get my license plate back. I gave him the money and got to work.

As I started looking over the books in the factory, the payroll and everything else I could find—and speaking with anyone who knew English—I discerned what was really happening. This plant manager, who had been so kind as to offer to recover my license plate, was robbing us blind. Not only had he been creating and paying dozens of fake employees, he was allowing the company to be overcharged on freight because his uncle owned a local freight business. In addition, his cousin was the customs agent, so everyone within a thirty-mile radius was getting handouts, kickbacks, and anything else that wasn't bolted down. Upon further investigation, I learned that he'd only given the local cop $100 to get my license plate back, so he'd stolen from me as well.

A bit of this is what you bargain for when you opt to do business in some countries, but your business is still supposed to come out way ahead after figuring in all of the unexpected extortion, bribery, theft, and hassle. In this case, the thieving plant manager was sending the entire business down the tubes. He did share one relevant tidbit with me: this company controlled 90 percent of the market in which it operated, and he thought the owners were naive for not hiking prices sooner. That, I admit, was welcome and appreciated information. Once I'd returned stateside, I raised the prices on our primary widget by 25 percent, quickly made the company profitable again, and sold it off in full. Needless to say, I also fired the plant manager and everyone he was doing business with, but none of those problems were mine after I'd sold the company—and recovered my license plate.

For me, this is all in a day's work. Over the course of my career, I've seen hundreds of millions of dollars in fraud, saved at least 100,000 jobs by laying off more than 10,000 people, renegotiated more than a billion dollars in commercial leases, left many billions in unpaid loans and debt behind me, and dodged 200 rounds of Uzi ammo and a couple of shotgun blasts to boot. This is my job. I'm a turnaround professional. I go into failing businesses and make them profitable again. What I do isn't always pretty, but it is effective. I keep companies once on the brink of collapse from their impending doom.

Thirty years in this business has left me with a lot of lessons, many of them about what not to do if one wants to run a business successfully. That's what this book is all about: learning from the mistakes of past CEOs.

I've always believed in giving back to the business world, whether through knowledge, volunteering, or my time. I give presentations to CEO groups, mentor local entrepreneurs, and do pro bono work for community organizations because I believe that they should all benefit from the lessons I've learned over the years seeing hundreds of failed businesses. If leaders can learn from the mistakes of others to enhance their own enterprises, institutions and organizations, save money, and avoid losing everything, that makes me happy. It makes me feel like I've contributed to individuals, communities, and economies, all of which better our homes, our countries, and our world. If I can talk to entrepreneurs who are growing their businesses and show them the mistakes that others have made, then I'm creating value for them and their families. This book is meant to provide as much of that value in the form of stories, advice, and lessons as I can possibly pack into these pages.

So what qualifies me to tell you about the mistakes that so many other CEOs before you committed and tell you that you should learn from their mistakes? Well, in the first place, I am the Turnaround Authority™. I can appreciate how that may not mean much to you yet, so let me tell you how I became the Turnaround Authority™. They don't teach Turnaround 101 in college or business school. I became the Turnaround Authority™ because of the business experience I've garnered over the course of four decades.

I started my career in real estate management in the early 1970s; I was immediately exposed to fraud and earned some of my earlier stripes in that department. I moved into banking shortly thereafter and found it fascinating to sit on the other side of the money. Being a banker allowed me to learn about the kinds of challenges and issues that made my boss or me knee-jerk, shut down companies, and fire CEOs. I began compiling my list of things that CEOs shouldn't do in relation to their bankers or their money, which I'll share with you in chapter 4. This is the other side of the table from where I—and probably you—sit now, but it's been nothing but a benefit to understand and appreciate what bankers, investors, and creditors are thinking when it comes to business, CEOs, and money.

Recognizing my predilection for creative problem solving and business resurrection, a company called Seaboard Industries hired me to start assessing their challenges. At Seaboard, I was shot at and defrauded, and you better believe I learned a ton. One of the directors at Seaboard asked me to do an assessment of another company for him, which gave me more on-the-job training and experience. My ability to assess and solve the problems of failing businesses ultimately led me to Grisanti, Galef & Goldress, a premier boutique turnaround firm that is the·oldest in the country. I eventually became chairman and under my tutelage, GGG won seven Turnaround Management Association Awards. What I've seen in my day, the experiences I've had, and the lessons I've learned have all made me the Turnaround Authority™, and it's with that knowledge that I sat down to write a book about the lessons you can learn from failed CEOs.

Let's suppose that your company is growing swimmingly. You hire more people every year, see increasing year-over-year profits, continue evolving and diversifying, growing and succeeding. Why should you care what I have to say about CEOs and the mistakes they've made at their companies? These companies weren't always failing, and these CEOs weren't always doing a poor job. Some of the companies that I've turned around were once worth billions of dollars, many worth tens and hundreds of millions. They had international operations, thousands of employees, enormous state-of-the-art facilities, factories and offices, and, at some point, stellar profits. But the good times didn't last, and in many cases the reasons can be pinpointed. Every case I deal with has its own set of nuances and requires its own turnaround plan, but after four decades I rarely encounter a unique lesson. CEOs in one industry face the same kinds of challenges and make the same kinds of mistakes as CEOs in other industries, in other places, and in companies of different sizes. The value of the lessons derived from their mistakes, therefore, transcends what makes them special or distant from you and the concerns of your company.

All businesses have relationships with their bankers, lawyers, boards, and advisors; all businesses have employees, cash flow, payroll, expenses, and "widgets", all businesses have competitors, market conditions, and exist as part of a larger economy. Though I never cease to be amazed at the innovative and creative ways that people steal, all business owners have to be concerned with fraud and how to protect their businesses from it. As a business leader, you can learn from the mistakes of past CEOs and implement concrete and actionable changes in your business that will protect you from making the same errors—or at least help you find solutions quicker and more nimbly than those who failed before you. As a CEO or business leader, you can grow your business safely with lessons from this book. Taking my advice and implementing actual steps in regards to the lessons I share will make your business run more efficiently and increase your profits.

This brings me to an important point: who this book is for. I've told you how much this book can benefit CEOs, yet it can bring tremendous value to many others as well. This book is for any business leader, including CEOs, presidents, owners, board members, senior staff, directors, and managers, to name a few. Business professionals like bankers, lawyers, and

> **You can learn from the mistakes of past CEOs and implement concrete and actionable changes in your business that will protect you from making the same errors.**

accountants will also benefit when equipped to dispense valuable advice to clients armed with knowledge about the mistakes of past CEOs. And you need not be a business leader to benefit from the lessons shared here. Any leader of an organization, from non-profits to community organizations, volunteer groups, or school clubs will find salutary advice in these pages. Moreover, employees, staff members, or anyone else who wants to learn to think like a leader will find a great deal of value herein. Yes, this book is filled with business stories, business terminology, and business problems, but these are, at their heart, the problems and challenges faced by leaders in general. The approaches outlined, the advice proffered, and the stories articulated are all meant to amuse, inspire, and make people think about how they can be leaders, whether they are now or aspire to be.

Entrepreneurialism is the backbone of every American enterprise and business, and entrepreneurs are the seedlings from which most great business leaders grow. I encourage every entrepreneur or aspiring entrepreneur to read this book and take its lessons to heart. Grow your business from the very beginning with this counsel and with these experiences fresh in your mind, and you and your business will have a leg up that many others do not have. I am confident that anyone who reads this book will find himself or herself on a faster career path because he will be better able to contribute to his organization, a fact that will surely be noticed by upper management (particularly if they've read Chapter 7 about communication).

Over the course of seven chapters we'll address far more than what follows, but I have grouped my stories, issues, and advice into seven main areas. The first three chapters span the trajectory of my most hardened advice for CEOs. Chapter 1 is all about checking your ego at the door, admitting mistakes, and figuring out who you are as a leader. The next chapter insists that you confront the harsh realities that face you and your business. You wouldn't believe how many CEOs fail because they refuse to acknowledge that they have problems in the first place, but it's how they should have dealt with those problems instead that is key. Chapter 3 is all about my business maxim: be proactive, not reactive. This chapter serves as a comprehensive evaluation of what a proactive leader does and does not do as well as those character traits that a proactive leader embodies. The next four chapters are about four large issues that should be of the utmost concern to those business leaders who are able to check their egos, confront their harsh realities, and become proactive. These chapters cover your banking relationship and money, how to avoid, prevent and mitigate fraud with the help of specific tips, how to understand and keep sight of the bigger picture in all facets of your business, and how communication and buy-in with your team members and key stakeholders are the keys to success.

Allow me to provide a few caveats. The first is about the CFO, a person/position that it may seem like I distrust, but that I do not. I will write a lot of things about CFOs who lied, cheated, and stole. I will caution you on multiple occasions to watch what your CFO is doing, to force him into a surprise vacation at erratic times, to review his work, and to question what he tells you. Upon reading these warnings and repeated requests, you may say, "Lee really hates CFOs," but that is inaccurate. Some of my closest friends, most trusted employees, and loyal confidants are and have been CFOs. My words of caution so often pertain to CFOs because they have the most access to the largest amount of money with the least oversight. Money is tempting. Money makes people act in ways they might not otherwise if they had access to less money with more oversight. It's an unfortunate reality of our business world and human nature. If CFOs come up in my cautionary tales as those to watch most fervently, it is only in proportion to the amount of money they control. You might keep a pet hawk because he's a great hunting companion, but you shouldn't be surprised at what may happen if you leave him alone with your pet rabbit for too long.

I've also had the pleasure to work with many CFOs who understand the turnaround process and knew how to fix their company. They were invaluable to me and deserve a lot of credit for their work.

I would also like to offer a caveat about gendered pronouns. You will notice that in almost all cases I use the pronouns he and him. I do not do this because I am sexist or because I don't recognize the value in gender equality or gendered pronoun equality. I do this because the overwhelming number of examples of CEOs and business leaders in my stories are men. That's simply the nature of my experience. If this bothers you, just remember that my stories are not just about men—they are about men who failed.

Names of people and companies are also something that I have considered while writing this book. I take client confidentiality very seriously, and I have taken every precaution to protect the anonymity of those whose names, companies, and shortcomings should be guarded. In certain cases, I have changed names and industries, and in others I have used fewer proper nouns, preferring instead to stick to words like "owner" and "company." Where information is a matter of public record, like in bankruptcy cases or more famous instances, I may use a company's real name or the names of people involved.

Finally, I want to address a staple of my vocabulary: widget. I use widget to refer to nearly anything that one can sell. It doesn't matter what you're manufacturing, assembling, developing, building, or selling, whether it's a physical good or intellectual property. If it can be reproduced and sold repeatedly, it's your or your company's widget.

Now, let's embark on this journey of the mistakes that CEOs make and the lessons you can learn from them.

Chapter 1

Check Your Ego

If you're not ready to check your ego right now, please close this book. I won't be offended. If you received this book as a gift, the buyer might be annoyed to have shared it, only to have you crack the cover, scan the introduction and set it down after the first sentence, but sometimes business investments aren't what we expect. It won't be the first time that someone took a loss before listening to me. My concern is not the monetary investment in this book. It's the mental one, and so my interest, at least at this moment, is your ego. In order to read this book—and truly benefit from it—you have to check your ego at the door (or in this case, at the cover).

I'm not suggesting that you shouldn't have an ego. After all (full disclosure here) I have a big ego, and it would be hypocritical of me to deny you the same pleasure. In my line of work a sizable ego comes with the territory, and I hardly think anyone with a diminutive ego would presume to write a business book filled with advice gleaned from CEOs' mistakes. Checking my ego, though, is a personal prerequisite of entering a business that needs my help, and to open yourself up to this book and take an honest look at your business, I want you to do the same.

As a turnaround professional, it's my job to recognize and understand what's gone wrong in a business so that I can restore it from the brink of collapse, make it profitable again, and return it intact to its CEO, board or whoever's left standing after the tough work has been done. However, I can't begin that process effectively until the president, CEO, or owner—whoever's in charge—checks his ego. It's essential to the turnaround process and the first step to admitting one's mistakes and thinking clearly enough to run a business successfully again. Only then can I learn enough about what's gone wrong to fix the problems facing the company.

Consider this a rehabilitative process for CEOs. I don't need you to journey along some 12-step program; I won't suggest that you surrender to a higher power or apologize to everyone you've wronged. If you were good at surrendering and apologizing, you likely wouldn't be the leader of a company. What I do need you to do, though, is appreciate that your ego may be responsible for some of the problems you're having (or at least their perpetuation) and that when you subdue it, you can admit your mistakes and fix them. An unchecked ego is the predicator of the crises that face many CEOs and blind them from resolving their larger challenges. So, check your ego and let's start learning from others.

The $8 Million Mistake

We all make mistakes. I make them. My friends and colleagues make them. Your employees make them, and yes, you make them. Mistakes are valuable because they teach us about ourselves as well as lessons for what not to do in the future. If you want to learn from past CEOs' mistakes, though, you must accept that you have, can, and will make your own mistakes, and that those mistakes have value as well. As an astute nineteenth-century author, Christian Bovee, once said, "It is only an error in judgment to make a mistake, but it shows infirmity of character to adhere to it when discovered." Exactly. CEOs' mistakes don't cause businesses to fail as much as CEOs' adherence to those mistakes. Even during a turnaround, each case requires mid-course changes to be successful, as most initial assessments and action plans are only half right.

When was the last time you made a serious mistake? How did you react when you realized the error? In our success and efficiency-oriented society, people often think of mistakes as shameful and to be ignored or hidden. Upon realizing their mistakes, many business leaders focus more on burying their errors and developing excuses than trying to repair the problems they created. Here's the official word on this: these leaders are wrong, and you should not follow in their footsteps. I've seen this approach implode more companies—or at least CEOs—than I can count. Do not bury your mistakes. Own up to them. The perception of our mistakes as leaders can be wisely managed, and we will truly be great leaders when we recognize that mistakes are opportunities to exercise leadership and set noteworthy examples, earning respect from our employees.

There was a particularly brainy CEO with a PhD I once replaced whose company manufactured electronics parts. In my estimation it was his educational background (read: book smarts, not business smarts) that augmented his ego so enthusiastically—and that was ultimately his undoing. As he reviewed his numbers one day, he discovered some cost accounting discrepancies in his books. Upon further inspection, it became clear to him that he was selling his primary widget under cost. He needed to "restate" his previous year-end numbers, which would result in a $2 million loss instead of what was previously considered a $1 million profit. He didn't notice these discrepancies due to quickly turning receivables and consignment inventory, a story for another time. Obviously his cash was out of balance too but was disguised by his foreign accounts and sticky-fingered controller. This was a good example of a much-needed year-end audit.

Embarrassed by his mistake, this CEO opted not to tell anyone, and simply to adjust his prices to profitable numbers. Let it forever be noted that glossing over mistakes is in and of itself a huge mistake.

Not only did this CEO fail to tell his banker what had happened (a serious lapse in judgment), but he also angered a number of his customers, who didn't understand the sudden 50 percent price increase. Desirous of protecting his ego, he chose not to tell them that the price hike was the necessary result of an accounting error, so to the further detriment of his business, this CEO lost these angry customers. Much as he may have been embarrassed, his customers would likely have understood this error and appreciated why he was raising prices as a result. They wouldn't necessarily have loved it, but they probably would have accepted it and continued purchasing from his company. Unfortunately, he chose to lose customers, credibility, and his business rather than admit his mistake. As his cash flow deteriorated from an extended period of selling below cost, his missing cash, and the subsequent loss of income from an eroded customer base, the bank noticed that there was a problem with his accounts and his ability to repay his loans. Had this CEO been honest with his bank and brought in a professional to manage the challenge, he would have remained the owner of his company and avoided a full-blown crisis. However, his ego interfered, his bank gave him the boot, and I was brought in to clean up the mess. The company was sold in four months, and the lender and creditor were paid in full. Unfortunately, the equity of the business was toast: $8 million down the drain.

Acclaimed business researcher and author, Jim Collins, notes that truly exemplary CEOs (what he calls Level 5 CEOs) often accept fault for all mistakes made at their companies, even and especially those that they did not make, recognizing that it is the person at the top who is responsible for all that lies under his aegis. I recommend you take that finding to heart, using his model of what makes an excellent CEO and my model of what makes a lackluster and flawed one, to improve your own ability to recognize and admit mistakes. There's no need to send a press release that discloses every error in judgment, but understand that those around you often know when you've messed up. Wouldn't you rather be seen as an upstanding leader, who acknowledged the flaw in his actions and proactively rectified his errors? That's what sets a stellar example at your company, and failing to set a good example is another classic CEO mistake that you should avoid.

Win the Game of Follow the Leader

Employees follow the examples of their superiors, whether or not either party intends for this to be so. Sure, employees have their own opinions and attitudes, and may behave with a greater or lesser degree of integrity, but at the end of the day subordinates follow their managers' examples. As CEO, set an example about admitting your mistakes. When employees make mistakes, they can often be rectified, but if you make mistakes and cover them up, employees will follow suit, and mistakes will be hidden until it's too late to fix them.

When employees see a manager or owner put cash straight from a register into his pocket, they will consider that acceptable. I recall numerous fraud cases in which plant managers justified taking inventory without the correct paperwork by noting that the president was doing likewise. If they hear a president bad-mouthing clients and customers, they will consider that the company's attitude—and follow suit. At one company, I read that one of its five core values was delivering an amazing customer experience that revered the customer above all else. This principle was elaborated upon in an extensive manifesto posted on the wall. When I visited their corporate headquarters, though, I heard people making snide remarks about customers and undermining the value of the customer's experience. How could this be happening when there was a poster on the wall delineating the opposite about their values? Finding that puzzling, I became a fly on the wall, only to hear the CEO and director of customer service talking derogatorily about some customers' problems. I'd found the reason. This was a do-as-I-say-not-as-I-do situation, and that doesn't work with corporate leadership. When the CEO and the head of customer service bashed the customers' issues, the rest of the employees felt comfortable doing so as well.

How employees receive appreciation and recognition for their work is important, because delegating responsibilities and sharing credit for a job well done is crucial to a company's success. When employees feel that they will be acknowledged for stellar work and shown the gratitude they deserve, they become that much more likely to admit their mistakes. On the contrary, if they don't receive credit for great work, then they won't want to be blamed for messing up. Knowing that quality work is praised makes employees understand that the company deserves to know when they've erred. Almost without fail, employees will follow the example that's set for them in this regard.

Mistakes will be made at all levels of every business; that's unavoidable. Cultivate a culture that makes room for personalities, experiences, and capabilities of all kinds, appreciating that different people contribute in different ways to success and an increase in the bottom line. Most companies don't have only super stars. They should seek them in the various game-changing positions (and you'll need to compensate them accordingly), but making sure all people feel appreciated is essential to creating openness and an environment that mitigates crises. Companies that promote an environment that sweeps mistakes under the rug will often find themselves facing problems that detract from the CEO's ability to grow the company. As a leader, you set the example people will follow, whether that example is fraudulent, against your company's values, or exemplary. I recommend you make it the latter.

Are You the Right Person for the Job?

Take a good hard look at yourself and recognize whether or not you are an entrepreneur or a professional manager. Both are important, but there's not often a great deal of overlap between these two positions in the same person as companies grow and get operationally complex. Think about it like this: you can't start a business without an entrepreneur, and you can't keep a business running successfully long-term without a professional manager. Recognizing the point at which your business requires the transition from a leader who is an entrepreneur to a leader who is a professional manager is crucial. The required transition may occur at the one million or $500 million dollar mark based on a company's industry, but it's guaranteed to occur. If a company is to thrive, not just survive, this transition must happen with a relative lack of disruption. Let me give you two examples, one in which the company's founder—a talented entrepreneur—has still not recognized that he desperately needed a professional manager, and the other in which a team of two entrepreneurs evolved so that one of them could be a professional manager while the other one remained an entrepreneur.

> **Recognizing the point at which your business requires the transition from a leader who is an entrepreneur to a leader who is a professional manager is crucial.**

Carl, the leader of a toy design and distribution company in Tallahassee, had a great idea for a series of innovative new toys. As he successfully developed those toys and built a company and brand around them, he cultivated relationships with other toy companies and began exclusively distributing some of their products as well. He developed more toys, bought high-quality, specialty equipment to better vertically integrate his operations, started selling his innovative products to a variety of middlemen distributors who placed them in toy stores, drugstores and all over the Internet, produced catalogs, and more. Sounds great, right? Well, it was in many ways but one: the CEO of this company was at heart and in action an entrepreneur and not a professional manager capable of recognizing when his company needed the latter. As a result, this toy company faced a number of acute challenges.

In the first place, expensive toys led this business to have a sharp annual earning cycle that peaked dramatically around the holiday season. Though the company was moving merchandise the rest of the year, it wasn't with nearly the same volume and gusto, and the cost of running the business was barely—if at all—covered during the rest of the year. The owner needed loans and investment to get him over the 9-10 month stretch outside of the holiday season. This challenge is true for many businesses, but it didn't have to be for this one, because the variety of product lines it carried could be successful year-round if other elements of the business were managed correctly. Carl is a creative guy, good at R&D and marketing, but he couldn't see that his business wasn't being managed successfully overall. Systems improvements, better staffing and personnel decisions, a better top-down focus, and many more issues that a professional manager brings to the table would make all the difference. Unfortunately, because the CEO still has not set his ego aside to recognize that he is not a professional manager and that he needs one, no one has been brought in to fix the problems, and every year the company holds on by a thread. In my estimation, it will only be so long before the business goes under if a professional manager is not hired.

On the other hand, I know of a two-person team that grew its business rapidly in its opening years. Though both members of this team thrived as entrepreneurs, were good at creative development and fast-paced innovation, they soon realized that as their business and team grew one of them needed to step into a more managerial role. They gave themselves the roles of CEO and COO. The CEO continues to lead the company through entrepreneurial-style development with the accompanying spirit, and the COO builds systems to govern their business. He became a manager for their employees and ensures that the operation they created continues to run smoothly. As it happens, their skill sets and approaches complement each other, making for a dynamic team and business. The fact that they had two people, each able to focus on a separate realm, throws into relief the challenges of a single business owner transforming himself from an entrepreneur into a professional manager. That's why there's no shame in recognizing that professional management is a challenge for you; if you come to this realization, bring someone else into your business to manage the show. You can often divide responsibilities to continue doing what you're best at and let someone else take care of operational and managerial responsibilities. A CEO who is a professional manager could be the best thing that ever happened to your bottom line.

Learn from Carl's struggles and those of many other CEOs. Recognize when you're not the right person to professionally manage your company, and hire a professional manager to grow your company like it did when it only needed an entrepreneur.

Leverage the Talents of Others to Your Advantage

I hire people who are smarter than I am. Rather than worrying about being the smartest guy in the room or the one with the best ideas, I concern myself with being a catalyst to get the job done. CEOs who have to be the best at everything often fail to delegate successfully or recognize when others' talents surpass their own. We each have our own specialized areas of expertise—skills that we can do better than other people, and those skills should be identified. Do you know what you're better at than most other people? Take a second to recognize your own specialties, particularly as they pertain to business, economics, finance, marketing, etc. While considering your talents, don't neglect to pat yourself on the back if you're also a great parent, spouse, or friend, or if you have a green thumb, a carpenter's right angles, or a mean curve ball. Whatever your abilities, I encourage you to identify them. Now that you've had a moment to think about what you're most adept at and revel in those skills' indispensability to your business, appreciate as a corollary that others have unique talents that you do not have, and which should be leveraged for the advantage of your business. Their talents do not diminish your own, and understanding this could be the key to your and your business's future success.

Business leaders who do not think this way—who insist on being the top dog intellectually or who have problems with other people making more money than they do—inevitably run into problems. Indeed, I was once brought into a company at which the CEO, Morray, could not stand that others would be perceived as more successful than he was in terms of power, responsibility, and money. Morray's initial goal was to capture the sales industry's top talent and effectively motivate that talent. He created a very generous sales commission structure, and true to his goal, he attracted an excellent sales manager and a very talented supporting sales staff. The sales manager, Vernon, performed swimmingly, meeting and exceeding goals and creating record revenues and profits for the business. Vernon made twice as much as Morray in his first year on the job. This agitated the CEO and caused him to put his personal interests before those of the company, asking the board for a raise. When the board refused to give Morray compensation greater than that awarded to the sales manager, Morray attempted to lower the sales team's commission structure, despite the latter's success on behalf of the company under the arrangement. This forced change to the pay structure served to dis-incentivize Vernon and his team, and the sales manager quit to work for a competitor. The board of directors discovered the CEO's blunder and fired him. Morray failed to utilize excellent talent and rely on key subordinates if such utilization and reliance challenged his ego. That cost him his job.

I want to know the weaknesses of any company I am hired to lead. (Think about the only-as-strong-as-your-weakest-link concept.) Have a frank conversation with your team about the weaknesses in your business. Because I'm engaged in businesses that are already facing crises, no doubt the immediate weaknesses are apparent, but it's an analysis of everywhere else that the company is fragile—and therefore vulnerable—that allows me to prevent further and future catastrophes that are most likely to strike when a company is already in critical condition. If I detect weaknesses, I can quickly reassign top talent or hire those who can handle the challenges, stop the bleeding, and move the company forward.

If I'm brought in to manage a company experiencing a cash crisis—like when payroll is due on Friday though there isn't enough cash to cover operations through Wednesday—but discover that a company's key products have not evolved in two decades and are now competing in a saturated market, that's a weakness that needs to be addressed and is no doubt linked to the cash crisis, or will be one day. If I learn that we have a Big Gorilla as a client (which I define as accounting for 25 percent or more of revenue, and which I'll discuss in greater detail in Chapter 6), then I'm going to move towards mitigating that potential crisis early. It's knowing these weaknesses that resolves current problems and staves off future ones.

There's little I find as useful in business as knowing my weaknesses or simply those tasks that others do better than I do. I try to surround myself with those people, employees, and colleagues who can do well what I cannot. Whenever I look for a new associate or partner for my own firm, I ensure that this person has skill sets and areas of expertise that are outside of what our firm already knows, does, and provides. In that way, our business model and its services grow and evolve, and we get stronger as a company. Many business gurus will tell you that your company should specialize in one core competency and be the best at that widget, service, or goal that it can be, and my advice is not meant to run contrary to that; I'm talking about people, not your business. Fill your business with people who excel where you are drab, and do this by knowing your weaknesses.

Don't Surround Yourself with Yes Men

As a turnaround professional, I am often the bearer of bad news. Yes, I fix things. Yes, I save my clients millions of dollars, their companies, homes, jobs, and livelihoods. And yes, my clients mostly like me in the long run. As it is, though, I am often the one to lay the reality on the table and declare that the best way to save a company is to, for example, close a factory, lay off 100 people, fire the owner's son, file for bankruptcy, or any number of other options that arise during a game of turnaround roulette. That's just the nature of my business.

It's not that each of these decisions and moves isn't necessary and ultimately for the greater good—layoffs and factory closings often mean the survival of a company and therefore its other factories and jobs—but it does mean that people look at me as the bearer of bad news because I am not a yes man. I do not tell clients just what they want to hear, as some of their other advisors may. I tell them what they need to know, though in some cases they already knew but just couldn't do what had to be done. That said, I sympathize with the reception of bad news and understand that accepting unfortunate circumstances and the resultant necessities doesn't mean liking either of them.

One particular moment stands out in my life in which I understood how my clients feel when I tell them the harsh solution to their problems. An advisor was explaining something to me that I wasn't thrilled to hear. I fell silent as I looked at my interlocutor, listening to his words. I couldn't help but give him the same look that my clients often give me when I articulate their predicament. He misperceived my silence for misunderstanding, though, and began anew to explain the situation. I cut him off and said, "I understand. I just don't like it."

It's obvious to say that understanding doesn't imply pleasure in agreement, but when we acquiesce to what we understand—agree or not—it's important to recognize the larger benefits that will derive from our tough choices. No one becomes a CEO because he likes making the easy decisions in life. Embrace those people who confront you with the harder decisions. In the long run, they strengthen your business and your character and deepen your experience. You don't have to like what they have to say, but it's a classic CEO mistake to shun them, especially during a crisis.

When Business As Usual No Longer Works

If there's a lesson that I hope you've started to derive from these pages, it's that change can be a good thing. If managed effectively, it often is. Progress is predicated on change, however resistant we might be to that change happening. Many CEOs are hardened against change, especially after many years as CEO of the same company. I find this ironic since any CEO who began his career as an entrepreneur (and who may still be one) likely started and built his company on a foundation of change: the desire to change an industry or the way a product was made or a service delivered. I can't think of a single business that didn't begin by setting out to change something. Nonetheless, as a business grows and becomes profitable, its CEO often becomes entrenched in his ways and increasingly contra change—almost scared of losing what he's already built—until he turns into a person slavishly committed to tradition for no better reason than, "We've always done it this way, so let's keep doing it this way."

Do not believe in continuing to operate in some particular fashion solely because that's what's always been done. Do not have sacred cows, especially not in business, and I encourage you to dispense with your pedestaled notions. Consider those ideas you've resisted integrating into your business because you've adopted an attitude of not fixing what isn't outright broken. You may find that a new and more welcoming attitude towards change is in order. When committing to enact positive

> **Every CEO must set aside his ego and involve his team in brainstorming, planning, and executing a new approach.**

change, assess situations subject to volatile conditions and seek creative solutions that quell a crisis and reenergize a company, pushing it back in the right direction. No CEO can do this alone, and no CEO can do this without embracing the value of change. Every CEO must set aside his ego and involve his team in brainstorming, planning, and executing a new approach.

When I go into a new company, that's one of the earliest actions I take. I explain to the directors, managers, board, and key team members that I'm not going to come into their company and pretend like I've brought all the good ideas with me. I'm going to need their help, and I have no pride of authorship. The overall message is that things have to change one way or another, that we will need our team's best efforts to enact that change, and that I need them to question me and talk to me about everything they do and know. I have an open door policy, and my team gets full access as long as they're prepared to change their company for the better.

Larry was the CEO of one of my most successful turnarounds to date: a seminar company. Larry was an amicable and jovial guy, and he loved nothing more than good news and happy tidings. In fact, he loved those things so much that he was unwilling to face his harsh reality and listen to team members and subordinates when they suggested that methods, processes, and the company overall had to change. Larry hated change, and it was Larry's inability to admit his mistakes and accept that change could be a good thing that led to the degradation of his business. At the seminar company, employees had been terrified into believing that change was wrong because Larry was so unwilling to listen to new ideas, much less change old ones.

Larry believed wholeheartedly that people were more likely to respond to registrations received in the mail more when they were postmarked locally. That is, if you live in Tennessee and you get an invitation from Vermont, you are less likely to open it and less likely to trust what's inside than if that same invitation was postmarked in Tennessee. As well founded as that hypothesis may be, I've yet to see the hard evidence that supports the theory, and the reality is neither here nor there when one considers how expensive it was to fulfill Larry's mail machinations. Larry insisted on posting hundreds of thousands of letters to people from their home states. He would have trucks drive hundreds of miles in every direction only to have all of the letters they were carrying postmarked in the state in which they were ultimately to be delivered. This cost the company about $400,000 annually, and it is only one example of ways the seminar company was hemorrhaging cash.

Do you think Larry's mailings are something I could have known about on my own upon first arriving? Absolutely not. A staff member suggested postmarking letters at the seminar company's headquarters to nix the expense of the trucks, gas, drivers, and hassle only after I convinced him and everyone else that I wanted to change the company's processes and procedures and do things differently. He'd tried to tell Larry this, but had been deterred by Larry's vehement opposition to change and his refusal to listen to the ideas of others. Whatever Larry had been doing at the company wasn't working or their EBITDA wouldn't have been negative $4 million and I wouldn't have been there. My insistence that people communicate openly with me and share their ideas for positive change was both a shock to the team and an essential factor in the success of the turnaround. CEOs need to embrace the idea of change and never stop evolving themselves and their businesses.

Drain the Swamp Before the Alligators Start Snapping

There's a classic saying that was once at the crux of our GGG advertising, and it plays through my mind to this very day: "If the alligators are snapping, it's too late to drain the swamp." Before we proceed with other lessons to learn from CEOs' mistakes, I want to explore the challenge of the alligators. Keep this idea in mind while running your business, as doing so may not only affect your profitability but your very survival. Here are a few examples of when the alligators are already snapping.

Consider the sales manager who is not producing what you've come to expect from him; you notice a decline in sales and even a disruption to the team. He should either be refocused or fired—but neither is done. Now your revenue and profits are down. If he handled your largest accounts and the competition is now selling to them, the alligators are snapping.

Your CFO is constantly late with financial statements, and the bank is growing concerned. You discover, after months of frustration, that he has personal problems that have affected his performance. Now the bank is questioning your ability to run your business and make the tough decisions. The alligators are snapping.

A typical survival story involves fraud. Almost half—yes, 50 percent—of our clients have encountered some kind of fraudulent situation. When the CFO/controller has been systematically stealing, or the plant manager is diverting inventory, the bank's knee-jerk reaction can leave you scrambling to find another bank. That's not easy to handle, especially when you're already reeling from the missing funds or inventory. The alligators are snapping.

When any of these scenarios—or hundreds of others—has arisen, draining the swamp is no longer an option. Draining the swamp would have been the easy way out of the scenario, an action to take before the alligators bite. A rising swamp represents the first signs of trouble on the horizon: the underperforming sales manager, the late financial statements, and the missing funds. Draining the swamp is recognizing the problem at these initial stages and handling it. By the time the alligators are snapping, you've got a full-blown crisis on your hands and draining the swamp just won't do. The alligators aren't just going to relocate and find another meal. You let them live in the swamp for too long, and now you have to face them directly. The alligators are a serious challenge to the integrity of your business and its survival. When they're snapping, you need to believe that you have a crisis on your hands.

If I had to offer a glib recommendation it would be to drain the swamp when there's still time, and that involves checking your ego and admitting your mistakes. It also involves being proactive instead of reactive, which is my number one rule for success. Create the kinds of controls, checks, and balances that regulate the processes of your business—and assess, analyze, and change them regularly—so that you are made aware of problems and can act on them long before the alligators start snapping. Ask lots of questions of your key people. Learn about your cash flow, your payables, and your company's projections; don't just believe what you're told. Follow up on the details and have an auditor check out those projections. Avoid the Big Gorilla, separate business from personal, get buy-in, and communicate. These are all subjects of future chapters, and though each may not individually drain the swamp, collectively they'll keep your business healthier and the alligators at bay.

Chapter 2

Confront Your Harsh Realities

You have a problem.

Don't deny it. Just acknowledge it.

I don't know what that problem is, but I have no doubt that you have one. Perhaps it's an employee who you once cherished but who has continually let you down in recent months. Maybe sales have dipped, and you can't put your finger on why. A recent marketing campaign may have flopped, or you may have some legal imbroglio or government agency barking up your tree. Sometimes it's a problem at home that's seeping into your ability to work effectively. Having a problem is not in and of itself a problem. The problem is not *acknowledging* that you have a problem. This is why one of the most important pieces of advice that I give is: *confront your harsh reality.*

One of the biggest mistakes CEOs make—whether or not they are in trouble—is refusing to recognize challenging situations. Often the test is to understand what issues might prove problematic in a worst-case scenario, as every crises is multi-faceted. Rather than being hidden, the problem is staring a CEO in the face, but he refuses to recognize it because doing so would mean having to handle it. Though tackling a big problem might seem taxing, I assure you that not dealing with it is worse. The following scenarios should get you thinking about whether or not you need to confront your harsh realities

Relationships with Your Vendors Have Deteriorated

It's late Friday afternoon, you're exhausted, and you realize that you've spent the entire week talking to your vendors. You're not placing orders or negotiating terms. You're not swapping stories; you're begging for extended credit terms. You're pleading for deliveries and making payment commitments without knowing how you'll pay the over-90-day balances. You're talking to the credit manager. If you're experiencing vendor fatigue, it's time to confront your harsh reality.

Cheerleader Supply specialized in cheerleading uniforms, pompoms, and accessories. More than 100,000 kids attended their various camps around the country. The company generated 65 percent of its annual revenue via its Christmas catalog, but UPS wouldn't deliver its catalog without a prepayment of freight costs due to the company's consistently broken promises about the payment of past-due invoices. With its annual revenue hanging in the balance and its catalog held hostage by a weary vendor tired of not getting paid in a timely and respectful fashion, Cheerleader Supply found itself faced with vendor fatigue. After the CEO decided to dig into his own pocket for the payments, the catalogs were shipped and the sales started rolling in.

The Superior Products Company of North Carolina had a similar problem. It manufactured oil products, and Exxon Chemicals supplied its key proprietary ingredient. Unfortunately, Superior Products was behind in its payments to Exxon Chemicals, and it was also in danger of losing a large packaging contract that it needed to make ends meet. There was not an economical alternative source for the additive Superior Products needed, but because of consistently broken promises about payment schedules, Exxon Chemicals denied Superior Products its key ingredient. The company couldn't recover and is no longer in business. This was a classic case of vendor fatigue.

Do not mess around with your critical vendors. Though you should always pay your bills, make sure that when facing a cash crunch you prioritize payments to those vendors who are going to keep your business operational. Your business may survive without copy paper for a month, hard as it might be, but you don't have a company if you don't have a product or service to sell. Critical vendors control some of the keys to your business's success, and you don't want to find yourself begging them to keep you alive.

Markets are Changing and Evolving and Your Business is Not

You once cajoled deliveries from vendors based on a promise, and you could make your promises reality. Not so anymore. Your core products look old and tired. Your website's most recent news refers to a four-year-old press release about a new salesman (who you fired three years ago). Worst of all, there's nothing new that you care to share. If you're out of new ideas, and the old ones aren't working, you need to confront your harsh reality.

Let me begin with an example of an organization that managed to evolve before becoming stale and continues to remain relevant to this day: the Centers for Disease Control and Prevention (CDC). The CDC was founded during World War II as the Office of National Defense Malaria Control Activities. Its sole job was to stop malaria. When malaria was no longer a threat in the United States, the organization that was to become the CDC didn't pack up and go home because its existence was no longer necessary. Instead, the organization evolved to deal with a host of issues related not only to disease control but also to disease prevention, and with this evolution it became nearly impossible for them to become outdated. The CDC is a great example of evolving to avoid stale ideas. Q-Zar, on the other hand, was a one-widget company.

Q-Zar, if you missed the mid-1990s, specialized in laser tag. When laser tag was created, it was phenomenal and fun, and used state-of-the-art technology. Q-Zar opened retail stores and laser tag arenas all over the country, enjoying a sea of rising profits. However, as the technology became dated and the market saturated when every big-box store carried a home-use laser-tag set, Q-Zar suffered. Undeterred by the increasing competition, Q-Zar stuck with its original idea. A pitiful attempt to rescue Q-Zar by a group in Texas that thought it could co-brand Q-Zar as a larger entertainment center with bowling, laser tag, paintball, putt-putt, and the like failed. The reason the deal fell through, though, is because Q-Zar found itself plagued by fraud and hadn't generated new ideas when it had the cash to support them. I'll tell you what I had to do to put Q-Zar out of its misery in Chapter 5.

Satellite dishes are another example of a banal idea. It's not that people don't still use satellite dishes, but the technology evolved faster than all of the companies that embraced satellites. There was a satellite communications company out of Marietta, GA called Satellite World USA that beamed information around the world. Because it was so heavily invested in this technology, it made one of its main lines the production, warehousing, and sale of enormous satellites. Satellite World USA didn't react quickly enough to the downsizing of the technology of satellites, and it had to sell the more profitable communications side of the company to support the stale idea that resulted in an excess of inventory in big, old satellite dishes. Don't get stuck on played-out ideas, especially if you're in the technology industry. If you have obsolete concepts or products whose lines naturally evolve quickly and you are not innovating in a changing market, you need to face your harsh reality.

Your Employees Are Losing Faith in You and the Company

Has that spark left your employees' eyes over the years? If the old-timers wonder where your magic went, and the newbies aren't sure how you ever got anywhere in the first place (are you even hiring new employees anymore?), you need to confront your harsh reality. I recall the egomaniacal and highly educated CEO who ran a computer parts company in El Paso, TX. His wife was his COO, and she will be forever known to me by the nickname her employees gave her: the Dragon Lady of El Paso.

When I arrived for my first day as Interim CEO, the bank had forced the CEO out because he was hurting more than helping and no longer thinking clearly about his problems. Moreover, the bank was aggravated by the CEO's lack of communication in the wake of a crisis. It seemed that a refusal to confront the harsh reality facing this Texan company was endemic to the leadership. The Dragon Lady, despite millions of dollars in losses and debt, was trying to save money by restricting the company's internal usage of toilet paper and coffee. You need to consider how crucial employees are to operations, and without toilet paper and coffee, I dare argue that they're less productive. I challenge any COO or CFO to demonstrate monetarily that restricting these items' usage effectively improves the bottom line. Needless to say, morale was at an all-time low.

When I arrived, the secretary came up to me and meekly looked into my eyes to ask if she could have $20 to purchase the daily allotment of toilet paper and coffee. Pause for a moment and think about that look: pitiful, defeated, and unmotivated. This is not the look you want in your employees' eyes. You don't extricate yourself from a crisis by restricting your staff's ability to stay alert and relieve themselves comfortably, and you don't rebuild a company with employees who have lost their faith in you and your leadership.

The King is dead. Long live the King. This single event changed morale and everyone worked together to save the company. It was financially stabilized and sold within six months with all employees keeping their jobs.

If your employees have lost faith in you, it's time to confront your harsh reality.

You are Working Longer Hours But Making Less Progress

You haven't had a vacation in three years. The lake/mountain/beach house is just a pile of cancelled checks and fond, but fading, memories. You're missing ballgames and ballet recitals with your children. You haven't had a nice dinner with your spouse since your anniversary, but maybe it was the anniversary two years ago. In the meantime, the inventory in the warehouse seems to be growing in size and dust. Are you working longer hours and making less progress? It's time to confront your harsh reality.

Digging yourself out of a situation like the one I just described is like trying to eat through an elephant: hard but possible, and as the old joke states, it can only be done one bite at a time. That takes prioritization. I find that CEOs who are spending more time solving fewer problems don't have a keen sense of the "bang for the buck" concept. In baseball, there are some hitters who are great at hitting singles, but when they swing for the fence, they're more likely to strike out. They need to understand the value of their time, which is well spent on a particular task and not so well spent on another. In the spirit of mixing metaphors and returning to our elephant, if you try to eat your way through an elephant in one huge bite, you'll choke. However, if you take one bite at a time or hit a series of singles—then you're likely to make your way through the elephant, or score a run. If you're drowning in metaphors, hours, and failures you need to prioritize and accomplish smaller things.

I worked with a company in Oklahoma that did refrigerator warehousing and freezer storage. The refrigerator warehouses needed repairs to run profitably, but the freezer storage was profitable without repairs—and with opportunities for growth. However, the CEO was neglecting freezer storage to repair the refrigerator warehouses. He continued investing cash and time into renovating and repairing the warehouses, whose continually decreasing margins were not worth the trouble. He was working more and had less to show for it. By simply refocusing the investment and time on freezer storage, which had higher margins and increasing volume to boot, I was able to immediately improve cash flow by implementing cost structure of refrigerated business to increase margins, which also contributed to the turnaround. I also worked on the overhead cost structure and fired the 88-year-old grandfather and chairman of the board who was earning $200,000 a year while spending most of his time in Naples, FL. The CEO had been spinning his wheels for months, working late into the night to get these repairs done and stay afloat, yet he made no progress. He needed to solve easier problems (signing up new freezer accounts, for example) instead of working hard to no avail.

Similarly, a sportswear company was manufacturing both domestically and overseas, but rather than profiting from both parts of the business, it was spending a fortune in money, time, and energy to improve the flagging overseas production. Because they'd invested so much money into this international operation, they couldn't bear to see it fail, yet they were limited by their cash position. This was the prisoner's dilemma: the more invested they were the harder it was to pull out, but they had to analyze the future from each point in time rather than bemoan the past. They were not destined to manufacture successfully overseas with the quality and consistency that their customers had come to expect, yet their failure only mounted as the company foolishly sunk more money and time into overseas production. Just like the refrigeration company, the CEO of this sportswear company was not facing his harsh reality: he was working longer hours for less progress. If you find this is happening to you, it's time to reassess your priorities. In each case, there was a sacred cow—the refrigeration side of the business and the international manufacturing—and I see this often. That's why it's my job to come into a company and shoot the sacred cow.

You are Stuck in a Vicious Cash Cycle

You're calling customers and finding they aren't paying because your shipments are late, wrong or incomplete—or maybe all three! Bankers' reference letters refer to your account as "low five-figure" as opposed to "high six-figure." You ask your CPA, attorney or friends for some advice on a new banker who understands this terrible economy/intense competition/horrible cost pressure better than the banker you've been with for ten years. If you have less cash, more debt, and an extended cash flow cycle then it's time to confront your harsh reality.

A printing company in the Midwest lost its largest account and was trying to make up for this Big Gorilla by selling more small jobs to less creditworthy companies. A vicious cash cycle ensued. As sales slowed and the CEO took on the additional risk of less credit-worthy customers to keep lines going and product moving out the door, he found that these customers paid slower than his Big Gorilla. This caused him to acquire an increasing percentage of bad debt reserve; his receivables were not collected quickly enough to pay his vendors. Unluckily though predictably, his vendors didn't care about these troubles. They simply wanted to be paid on time. He borrowed more money from the bank to keep his vendors happy. This bumped his credit line so that when he went to ask for additional money from his bank, they grew concerned because the books no longer reflected the company with which they'd initially dealt. Ultimately, this created—as it always does—a cash crunch.

The story of this printing company is not uncommon. It's so common that nearly all the companies that I go into have faced some comparable version of this vicious cycle. The challenge then becomes taking proactive steps to unravel the cash crunch and return to normal business operations. A professional CEO or CFO should see the signs early and not fall into a cash-flow trap.

You Have Lost Track of Your Personal Guarantees

Most entrepreneurs guarantee credit cards, real estate, leases, and more. Are you personally guaranteed on anything related to your business? How many personal guarantees have you signed that are still in force? If the answer was, "None, I think," I'm more concerned than if you'd said four or five because now I'm wondering how many there really are. Did you read to the end of every document you signed? Do you have an American Express business card? Do you have a business loan from a bank? Do you process credit cards? What agreements have you made for your business?

Most CEOs sign personal guarantees without keeping track of what they sign. Personal guarantees stipulate that if something goes south with your business, you will stake your personal assets on making sure those invested can recover their losses. So, if you have a business that one day goes belly up—even though in my experience these aren't "one day" situations but long periods of strong indicators that were ignored – the bank or whomever you have a personal guarantee with has a legal right to try to recover its losses by going after your personal assets. Depending on the personal guarantee, that means your money, your home, or anything else you own (I've seen yachts, prize-winning horses, and more go to those holding the strongest personal guarantee signed by the owner of a failed company). I've also seen way too many divorces and two suicides of those who were losing everything.

> **Most CEOs sign personal guarantees without keeping track of what they sign.**

If your business goes under, you don't want to lose everything you have. I've had numerous clients insist that they weren't personally guaranteed and that I shouldn't worry. Inevitably, when we sit down with all of their paperwork and go back to the establishment and conception of the business, we find personal guarantees owners didn't know they had or that they didn't think were still in force. But they were wrong, and they were at risk. One CEO said to me, "Oh, they can't take my house. That's in my wife's name and she never signs anything." Sorry, I told him, after taking a closer look—it appears as though she signed this. One thing I've noticed is that the older a business is, the more likely it is that the owner (who is also often the CEO or president) has personal guarantees that he's forgotten about. While working on one 25-year-old company at which Tom, the owner, was in a mess with his vendors, I sat around a large conference table consulting with the creditors and drafting plans for how we would restructure Tom's debt, reschedule a payment plan, and get everyone paid off fairly and appropriately, even if not in full. This agreement would produce greater results than a bankruptcy. I had the consent of an entire room—people nodding at me that they would ultimately take less money than they were supposed to receive—except one guy.

This older gentleman sat at the far end of the table clutching a grubby, worn document in his lap. He was frowning at me throughout this entire meeting, glaring down on me and never once nodding in agreement. I gave him a look of understanding: a look that said, Please be quiet, and I'll deal with you later. After the meeting, when everyone had left, I walked over to speak with him. He unfurled a 25-year-old document and flipped it to the last page, revealing a personal guarantee signed by Tom that would allow this single creditor to ruin our out-of-court plan. This man said very clearly that this personal guarantee was still in effect—he was right—and that he would not compromise on a single cent. He would not make waves with the others' plan, but he would expect to be compensated in full as stipulated in all original agreements and backed by this personal guarantee that allowed him to go after not just Tom's business but Tom's personal assets. Fortunately, he was the only one who leaned back on a personal guarantee, but had more creditors done this I would have had to negotiate Tom out of this ruinous document and similar ones at far greater cost to him and his business.

I want to encourage you to be as hyper-vigilant as possible when signing documents because personal guarantees appear in all kinds of places—and in some where they seem relatively innocuous. I recently had a client tell me that when he was setting up credit card processing for his business, the merchant bank wanted him to sign a personal guarantee for any customer charge backs. If he didn't pay his bill monthly—a simple, low, regular bill, mind you—then he would personally guarantee them the recovery of what they believed was due them (and the recovery costs, which would probably have been ten times the cost of the bills). The structure of the arrangement was one that already allowed the merchant bank to withdraw money at its leisure from my client's bank account. The merchant bank would not relent on the personal guarantee, though, and so a more mutually agreeable solution had to be found. In this case, we're not talking about being out a lot of money, but if this contract had a personal guarantee then imagine what other contracts you've seen and signed have in them.

Personal guarantees do serve a purpose—if your business lacks credit or represents an investment risk, it is understandable that those loaning you money want to be assured somehow. If, on the other hand, your business has been around awhile or the business relationship is less serious (e.g. a low monthly bill rather than a lease), reconsider before signing any personal guarantees and think about extricating yourself from those you're currently in. It always pays to think creatively. For instance, my client told the credit card processor that he would sign a limited personal guarantee that was only in force for one year. If he paid his bill on time every month for one year, then the personal guarantee would automatically fall off of the contract without any additional signatures or acknowledgements. The year, they agreed, would sufficiently prove that he was responsible and his business was credit-worthy.

Another client was leasing a large warehouse and retail "flex space" and due to the investment by the property owner in preparing the space, the latter wanted a $50,000 personal guarantee to last the duration of the five-year lease. Rather, we negotiated a $10,000 personal guarantee that stepped down over the course of the first three years of the lease. The existence of a personal guarantee made the landlord feel better, and we kept it to an amount that wouldn't be ruinous to my client if business turned south. Remember that if the point of a personal guarantee is to mitigate the risk of the person whose money, time, or property is on the line, then once you prove that you are credit-worthy, there is cause to argue for a removal of that personal guarantee.

You don't want to be at risk personally, or at least not more than you have to be, so try to get out of your personal guarantees, and don't sign them in the first place if you can avoid doing so. Just imagine over the course of three decades in business how many you could have signed if you weren't paying attention or didn't know what to look for: vendors, creditors, banks, investors, landlords, and the list goes on. Now is as good a time as any to review all of your paperwork in order to figure out where you're personally guaranteed. If your business is successful and profitable, not in debt, and established enough to no longer need the guarantee of your personal assets then it's time to renegotiate. You might be able to rework the documents on your own with your banker or in an hour with your lawyer or friendly neighborhood turnaround manager. If you have a host of personal guarantees, it's time to face your harsh reality and do something about them.

Politics are Crippling Your Company

All organizations have politics. Whether a 50,000-person enterprise, a non-profit, a school, a small business, or a social club, there will be politics.

The challenge you have as a business leader is to minimize the drama created by internal politics so it doesn't cripple your company.

Everyone has an agenda. Even keeping one's head down and doing a job for the paycheck is an agenda. So is sucking up to a boss for a promotion. But those are ordinary, personal-level agendas. Although this individualism could represent the culture of a company where the aggregate of these low-level politics could be an impediment to a strong business, these are not the politics that concern me because a better example can be set for them. I'm concerned about the kinds of destructive politics on the senior level that paralyze the operations of a company. Key decisions are made at the management level, so when senior leaders jockey for their political interests, they are making—or more likely breaking—their companies.

At one large company I turned around, there were some long-term directors who wanted to continue in the manufacturing business, while other directors preferred to morph into a licensing company; the former believed that they could still salvage their previous efforts, and the latter wanted to focus the company's remaining resources on a path that looked more promising. Even though the transition to a licensing company had already begun, the politics among these officers resulted in a six-month loss of time—not to mention millions of dollars— before the company pulled together on the project that would save them. It was this political jockeying without strong leadership from above that resulted in the need to bring me in to align everyone's interests and proceed in the direction that would save the company. A disagreement among board members is a healthy way of fleshing out the best ideas—and a normal process. However, everyone must truly have the best interests of the company in mind, as problems arise when a board member or senior manager tries to undermine the process of normal negotiations and discussions by currying the favor of senior management or board members who skew assumptions and strategies towards their desired outcomes. I've seen numerous companies disintegrate for these reasons.

As a company leader, it's your job to minimize the politics around you— and to recognize when you're the culprit in creating those politics. If you, as a manager, see politics that are not in the best interest of the business, you need to speak directly to people about their actions and emphasize that by working as a team, everyone is working towards the same goal: the success of the company. The bigger a company becomes, the more layers of management are created and the more political the environment gets. No matter how big your company grows, try to keep your business from becoming too political. The largest barrier created by politics is that the CEO is unable to get the right answers and information he needs quickly enough to act, particularly during a crisis. Even when a company is healthy, internal politics create unnecessary hindrances to honest communication and collaboration, but when a business is facing a crisis, politics always result in a slower turnaround. If you have a problem with politics and factions, confront your harsh reality and confront the members responsible.

You Don't Have the Right Management Team

Some CEOs make the mistake of trying to grow their businesses without a sufficient or competent management team. I took over leadership at a California-based brand that was popular in the 1990s. The company's ambitious directions repeatedly seemed to outshine the capabilities and strengths of its management team, a reality demonstrated by the fact that I had to run this company on two separate occasions. The first time I was brought in to refocus the company because it was in the manufacturing and distribution business and expanding overseas without the proper personnel who understood sourcing and distribution in international markets. Though the business lost a ton of money before our team arrived, we were able to end the capital hemorrhaging by scaling back, and eventually eliminating, manufacturing, and refocusing the company on design and licensing. Had they had the kind of management team in place that understood the nuances of international expansion and management, they would never have needed me.

Many years later my partners and I were brought back in for similar reasons. Not only had the company lost control of its brand, entered into poor licensing arrangements with substandard manufacturers, and become embroiled in trademark issues, but it had accumulated significant amounts of debt. Once again, the management team couldn't handle its responsibilities. I had to renegotiate licensing agreements, default substantial licenses, and bring focus back to the company's singular asset: a fantastic design department. Learn from this company and don't embark on new strategies for growth without acquiring the right management team first.

You Don't Have Enough Cash

This is a harsh reality indeed! Cash doesn't solve all of our business problems, but it covers up a lot of systemic ones. When businesses are profitable it's easy to ignore the places where cash is leaking; it's only when the cash cycle tightens that companies start to feel the pinch of reckless wastes of money. Vigilance in good times is essential. Ask all vendors for a discount on bills paid within ten days, review monthly bills to ensure that you still use the service or product you're paying for, and look at places to fine-tune and save on your production processes and freight costs. Profits cover problems, and I've never had a business call me because of a crisis in cash surpluses, but when that cash crunch hits, you'll wish you hadn't left money on the table during more prosperous times.

The discovery of a cash crisis requires immediate action: pump the breaks on what you think is necessary and regular spending, increase margins, and liquidate unnecessary assets. In nine out of ten cases, CEOs and their senior management teams tell me that they knew there was a cash-flow problem before they had a cash crisis and brought me in, and I always ask, "Why didn't you slow spending at that point to create a cushion?" The two most common answers are: 1. I thought it would resolve itself, and 2. because everything I'm spending is necessary. Both of these answers are incorrect. Cash-flow problems do not magically resolve themselves and it is never necessary to spend all of the money you have. I can always find ways of cutting back on spending.

Turnaround 101 dictates that you stop the bleeding as quickly as possible. Cash is spent for the best bang for the buck until everything is under control. However, timing can dictate a less than sophisticated procedure by slashing all spending by at least 15 percent. Tell every division, department, and agency that it needs to cut its cash needs—no exceptions. In this way, the pain will be shared across the entire company. There will be an enormous amount of pushback. There always is. The response is simple: "Do you want your company to survive until tomorrow or do you want to quibble about getting money that we don't have? Either cut 15 percent of your cash needs immediately or don't get paid on Friday." This is a tough path, but if you're spending $100,000 a month and save 15 percent, and $15,000 is going to ensure that you get an essential piece for your only profit-generating widget—like, say, the key ingredient from Exxon Chemicals—or pay a high enough percentage to some creditor to keep it from suing you for 90 days, then you cut 15 percent of everyone's spending. This kind of mandatory budget cut provides time to fine-tune operational requirements based on any improved results, but it is also solid management thinking: cut expenses to free up cash. Unless you work on the top line—the revenue line—of your P&L, too, however, then your efforts will be for naught. You need to make your operation run lean while growing margins and revenue. Taking these actions simultaneously is crucial to a successful turnaround, and doing them while creating cash flow is key.

So how does one create cash flow out of thin air, and extra time, too? Let's suppose that I'm going to create a million dollars in cash flow. To do this, first imagine that you have 30-day terms with your vendors, as that's standard, and a million dollars in payables every month. To simplify, I want you to just consider the first four months of the year: January through April. Over the course of those four months, the total outlay of cash is four million dollars: a million dollars in each month of January, February, March, and April. I'm going to make the $4 million dollars in payables due between January 1 and April 30—$3 million dollars for the same period. The secret is extending your normal trade terms from 30 to 60 days. By making that happen on the dot of January 1, suddenly your cash outlay for January is zero dollars! That means that the million dollars walking out the door in January is still in your pocket. In a cash flow equation, a million dollars has just been added to the positive side. If you can't extend for thirty days, do it for fifteen, thereby extending your payment terms and improving your cash flow. Any cash flow improvement is better than none.

Now don't misunderstand. You still owe that million dollars; no one gifted that money back to you. What we did was change the timing of your payments, so that they've been pushed back for every month going forward. Imagine what you could do with that million dollars if it wasn't owed in the month of January. This is certainly a good place to start recovering from your cash-flow troubles. Maybe the problem was generated by a long-term loan that came due and for which you didn't have the necessary capital. The repositioning of your terms has now created that cash flow.

Why have I just revealed one of my greatest tricks and one of the best strategies of my turnaround success? Because my real talent as a turnaround professional is playing Let's Make a Deal. I've been nicknamed the Monty Hall of Business for good reason. The key—and the challenge—to this strategy is doing the right financial assessment and then rapidly renegotiating with vendors to obtain extended terms and create that improved cash flow—all at the same time. This comes down to trust, reputation, and good planning. When businesses try to convince vendors to extend an extra thirty days to pay a million dollars, these vendors often become agitated and concerned. My job is knowing what vendors need to hear; making them comfortable; providing them with the proper assurances and at times collateral or personal guarantees; explaining the improvements to the business plan; or putting the company into play for a quick sale. I then ensure that those thirty days are used in the best possible way. Remember, you have to keep to your negotiated deals. Nothing creates vendor fatigue faster than broken promises. You don't ever want something like this—a massive renegotiation of terms—to blow up in your face, and it takes a professional to see this process through to the end. The other thing I want you to consider that's created through this strategy is the time. In business there's hardly anything so valuable as creating time, especially during a crisis, which by its very nature is time sensitive. My goal in sharing this strategy is not so that you go give it a whirl, but to show you that until you confront the harsh reality of a cash-flow crunch, you can't begin to fix it.

Your Employees Know More Than You Think

Have you ever thought to yourself, my employees have no idea what I make, or they have no idea what our profit is, or they have no idea what our secret formula is, or they have no idea what the password to my computer is, or the secret code on the alarm system? Well let me be the first to inform you: they know. There are few secrets—if any—in a company. Your employees know most everything. If you've ever thought, I hope they don't know, you better hope the information is CIA, level-5 classified, 90 percent expunged, kept in a safety deposit box whose only key you swallowed. Because if not, your employees know.

I once took over a warehousing company and began my job by dramatically slashing the owner's salary, which was not simply too high for the owner of a failing company 120 days past due in payments to the bank but too high for the owner of any company that size. I also fired his 83-year-old grandmother because she didn't do much more than knit the CEO socks for Christmas. Later that afternoon I was surveying the warehouse, which was a mile away from the offices and headquarters. A forklift driver pulls up alongside me and says, "Congratulations on firing grandma and cutting the boss's salary—he should never have been making so much money when we were past due with the bank!" Not only did this random forklift-driving employee already know that I'd taken both of these steps, but he knew what was happening in the first place. I'm telling you: your employees know.

If there is information that must truly be kept secret, think long and hard about who has access to that information, what computer(s) it resides on, where it is discussed and so forth. Despite the fact that tons of people at Coke must somehow or another work on or around the secret formula for Coke, I believe that this secret formula is still aptly named and just that: a secret. The reason is not that people at Coke aren't blabbermouths or that Coke has required every employee to sign what amounts to one of the most airtight and well-enforced non-disclosure agreements ever penned, but because Coke uses absolute discretion in the distribution of the specifics of its secret formula. Only certain people know certain things about the formula and are responsible for certain parts in the process of making the formula. I would imagine that only a handful of people know everything and that the official recipe is kept tightly under lock and key.

Ill-Chosen Family Members are Running the Business

One of the biggest mistakes that CEOs make is mixing their business lives with their personal lives, which includes employing family members. Personal and business just don't mix—at least not successfully. Without written expectations and a timeline for control, advancement, and responsibilities, putting family members in key positions of your business can be dangerous. It takes a unique parent or spouse and CEO to balance the intersection of a family and a business. Problems arise in many places, but particularly as it comes to entitlements, compensation, selling the business, and tax issues related to inheritance. There always seem to be expectations on either side that are not compatible. The number one way of avoiding these challenges is by putting everything in writing. Even so, entitlements can and do interfere.

Leaders, even good ones, have a surprising predilection for putting inadequate and ill-prepared family members in charge of key parts of their operations. Napoleon installed his family members as heads of state across Europe (for the most part, they were failures), and monarchy for millennia have been based upon familial succession. There's a good reason that none of these monarchies remains (and I'm not interested in the royal families of Britain or Monaco—these are just sustained wealth and fairytale fantasies): at some point every family breeds idiots. In the case that a son is as capable or more so than his father, that rarely lasts for a third or fourth generation. Sure, people can be groomed and educated, but at some point, the son may like other things, be less capable, or simply not care. None of those qualities is in and of itself bad, but each is bad for your business.

If you want to build a company that is sustainable, don't make your offspring a prerequisite of leadership. I'm not saying your progeny can't be involved, but you better make sure that they're both capable and desirous of the position and privilege. It's far easier to inherit something great than to build it, but in most cases only those who build truly know what it is to want and work for an empire. One place that problems tend to arise when fathers and sons do business together is in compensation, especially when selling the business.

I led a mechanical engineering company in New York through a restructuring that included dealing with a large union shop. The father had died and his wife was put in charge as interim CEO. She had two children and installed the younger one, her daughter, as CEO. The son, resentful of his diminutive role due to a lack of delineated expectations and a board-approved succession plan, and, in his eyes, inadequate compensation, was stealing to get his just inheritance. As a family member, the son felt entitled to the business's money, no matter how much or little he'd worked (and it was definitely how little in this case). When we confronted him, he attacked his mother with a kitchen knife. Fortunately, she lived, got a restraining order, and kicked him out of the company. Unfortunately, we were in the middle of selling the company, and this charade ruined the sale.

Mixing business and family is not easy. Be careful, and have the sense to know when someone is incapable of doing the job he feels entitled to do, family or not. In addition to ruining your relationship, your other employees always recognize who the weak links are, and they will lose respect for you and motivation for growing your business if you put an incapable family member in charge of something he shouldn't be. I'd rather you pay a family member not to work than to be disruptive to your operation, Although it may not be good parenting, subsidizing a spoiled brat's life rather than bringing him into your company is better business practice. If you value your business and key employees and respect your family, then think long and hard before involving children and family members at the leadership level. If you do and it's affecting your company, confront that harsh reality.

The CEO Can't Keep It Zipped

I have more examples of this harsh reality than any other problem I know of, but I'll keep my stories to a select few just to demonstrate how easy it is to get caught and how ruinous that is. The most public case of a world leader not keeping it in his pants concerned President Clinton. His failure to keep it locked down had to do with so many issues: his ego, his self-esteem, his power, and the simple urges of men. Interestingly enough, it's these same forces—ego, self-esteem, power and manly urges—that drive men to start companies and become presidents in the first place, but that's no excuse. Women are not off the hook on this one, as I have stories about them, too.

If for no better reason than to avoid getting caught (and better reasons include the sanctity of marriage, practical morality, metaphysical morality, putting your family or business first, etc.), do not cheat on your spouse while running a company. Don't cheat anyway, but please know what a bad idea cheating is when you're running a company, especially a public company. Or country. You will, eventually get caught, and the likelihood and timing of that calamitous outing has a shockingly strong correlation with the degree to which your company is facing a crisis. That is, infidelity has a way of rearing its ugly head when the business isn't the only thing headed south.

The president of a pipe manufacturer had other interests: he wanted to design the perfect hydroplane racer. He succeeded in crafting a racer with an innovative design, and he and his new racer were photographed for the cover of a prestigious industry magazine. However, during the cover shoot, he failed to ask his girlfriend to get off the racer or at least cover up her revealing bikini. When his wife saw the cover of the magazine and put two and two together, she filed for divorce and the president lost control of the company. After all, the business was started with his wife's father's money.

In another case I was brought in as Interim CEO where the former CEO and chairman of the board of a retail establishment had been caught with his kids' babysitter while his company was going through a Chapter 11 restructuring. Fortunately, as she was a senior in high school and of legal age the charges weren't as bad as they could have been, but once the matter became public, he lost focus on the business, and the employees and the creditors lost faith in him. Ultimately, this fifty-year-old business was sold off in pieces.

Another quickie, so to speak. A company was going through bankruptcy, and I was brought in to see it through the process. One thing I discovered while reviewing the books was a charge for a $75,000 diamond ring. Now, I hope you already know that it's not a good idea to purchase personal property on the company credit card, but during a bankruptcy such actions are illegal. As it happens, the ring wasn't even for the CEO's wife—it was for his girlfriend!

All three of these men lost everything—businesses, money, families, and the lives they had built. In summary, understand the consequences of infidelity at work. You will get caught, and it will not end well for you or your business.

I promised a few stories about women as well. I once worked with a female CEO in the oil distribution business in Texas. After she placed a hedge that she was prohibited from doing by the bank and it went bad, she had to restate her financial statements for the past two years. She tried to get out of it by propositioning the banker to get her loan renewed. It didn't work. That's how I became CEO.

Another female CEO of an apparel company in North Carolina liked the ladies and enjoyed going to strip clubs. She took her national sales manager to one, and caught up in the atmosphere I suppose, she got in on the action and performed a lap dance. She got fired. But I think she got to keep all the one-dollar bills.

When I became CEO of an auto parts chain in the Northeast, the marketing manager asked to speak with me on day one. She told me she'd been having a confidential affair with the former CEO for five years. Then she added that she was up for another five-year relationship. I informed her it wasn't too confidential and found a new manager.

While I was doing a month-long assessment of a huge company I found out some things about a female executive that she didn't think were material and didn't want reported. I disagreed. Sleeping with your largest vendor's president is not considered good business practice.

So she propositioned me pretty hard, even offering a weekend getaway with her to Paris on the company jet. Rather than take her up on the offer, I countered with an offer of thirty-days severance and had her escorted to her office to clean it out.

You Don't Know Where Your Business is Financially

It can be very easy to neglect your financials and just assume that all is well, as long as you're making payroll, the lights are on, and no tragedies are coming your way. That's not the kind of attitude that protects and grows your business, however. If you don't know at every moment where you are financially, then you're already lost. There may not be a major problem waiting for you in your books, but this sort of neglect happens over years as a business grows, as more layers of management are created, as bonuses are paid out and as the hands-on CEO becomes less focused. There are many reasons why CEOs don't know about their businesses' financial states. Whether it's because their CFOs or COOs handle the finances and day-to-day operations or they're semi-retired, all CEOs must have a thorough and regular concept of their businesses' financials to ensure that they're turning a profit—and not just the profit they think.

> A common mistake that CEOs make is creating a budget at the beginning of the year and thinking that hitting the numbers of that budget equals success.

A common mistake that CEOs make is creating a budget at the beginning of the year and thinking that hitting the numbers of that budget equals success. That's not always so. For instance, let's say a CEO projects a million dollars in sales each month and a 10 percent margin, or $100,000 in profit. Each of the next twelve months that happens, and the CEO is happy and believes he's making the numbers. However, in month thirteen—and I see this far too often—the company does a million dollars in revenue and makes $1.98 in profit. Profits don't pick up in succeeding months. What happened? The CEO was looking at the top and bottom lines of the P&L, and because those numbers worked, he was lulled into complacency. He wasn't looking at the roadmap that was meant to generate profits of 10 percent on a million dollars in revenue, and the product mix was changing, the margins on key products were getting tighter, and even though numbers balanced out, they eventually went sideways. Had the CEO been aware of where he was financially, rather than just looking at the top and bottom lines, this would have been less likely to happen. Driving from point A to point B can take many twists and turns. By only looking at the top and bottom line, the CEO lost track of the correct route.

The key is not just to review your financial documents, but also to act on the information you garner. If possible, involve your accountant and/or financial advisor and think about your budget, your taxes, and your opportunities. Involving and leaning on the advisors around you is a great way to confront your reality and subsequently and most significantly, to create ways of dealing with it. If other people have great ideas they'll be hard pressed to share those with you if you don't involve them in a candid financial discussion with accurate numbers. The harsh reality may be your burden to bear, but the CEO is not the only person at a business who is affected by the reality or who affects it.

Confront and Resolve Your Problems Early

Do any of the problems in this chapter sound like your reality? Have they been or could they be? These are just a few examples that my past clients have failed to recognize until their banks, investors, or boards of directors forced them to talk to me, or someone like me. None of these situations are ones of which you or others should be ashamed. They are often caused by outside economic issues that drastically affect your business. Though you can't anticipate them all, you must be prepared to react quickly and nimbly. When business goes bad, shame fuels the flames of your ego, keeps you from admitting past mistakes, and recognizing that change can be good.

As I mentioned, your reality may not be quite as bleak as some of these scenarios, but I have no doubt that there is a reality that, if confronted, you would be better off. Maybe it's as simple as an inventory management issue. Perhaps you run out of stock too frequently on some of the items in your warehouse and have to call your customers to let them know that shipments are going to be running a little late. It's not that you can't pay for the merchandise; it's just that you can't accurately forecast your need, track what you have, and organize your warehouse. Maybe you just have slow or difficult vendors. No matter the reason, this creates other problems and taxes on your business. Your processes may have worked in the past when you were smaller, but the current systems are no longer cutting it. This is not the same harsh reality that needs confronting as when you're ducking visits from your banker, but it is the kind of situation that I've seen many a CEO ignore for long enough that it negatively impacts his bottom line in wasted time, energy, and customer loyalty. It may not seem harsh, but it's a reality best recognized and handled immediately. Don't let problems linger: that breeds crises.

No one calls me and says, "Lee, I'm going to have a problem three weeks from Thursday." They say, "Lee, I couldn't make payroll this week, the bank is cutting my line of credit, and I have a half-million dollars in payables ninety days past due." By the time I'm invited to the party it's a full-blown crisis. Respect your problems by confronting and resolving them head on and early. It may be unpleasant in the moment, but you'll be glad you did, and you're much more likely to stay in business once you have.

Chapter 3

Be Proactive, Not Reactive

My singular guiding principle is to be proactive, not reactive. I live and conduct business by this axiom.

If there's one thing I know, and something you've surely experienced as a business leader, it's that all businesses have problems. Little goes exactly as you expect it to. If you're proactive in your leadership, decision-making, and planning then you'll have the tools, people, and ideas in place to handle much of what comes at you. On the contrary, if you're constantly reacting to everything, you'll never get your feet underneath you long enough to resolve your problems and prevent new ones from arising.

CEOs facing crises are most often reactive rather than proactive. In a crisis, events move far faster than usual, and the problems that arise are more unusual, making them more challenging to manage. Rather than play offense by scheduling meetings with bankers, lawyers, accountants, directors, and managers, many CEOs act like deer caught in the headlights. Deer do not manage businesses well and mostly get hit by cars and die.

As a CEO or business leader you must ask yourself, "Am I constantly reacting to business challenges, or am I being proactive to minimize problems?" This question has nothing to do with crises and everything to do with regular business management, which is why it's such an important lesson to learn from the mistakes of past CEOs. As you ponder this question, be honest with yourself. Do so by picking a specific example; for instance, consider the last problem your business faced.

Let's say that the last problem you had was a string of orders shipped out that customers complained were incorrect. This sort of thing happens sometimes, no matter how well your employees are trained and despite the checks you put in place through the processing and picking in your warehouse. However, if this is not an isolated instance but a string of incorrect shipments, then you need to look more carefully and ask yourself, "Are you reacting to this issue or have you already been sufficiently proactive such that the issue will resolve itself?" If you have twenty people in your warehouse and no way of assigning a particular person to a particular package—like, for example, having the picker and packer stamp packing slips with their names—then you will have a challenge determining responsibility. If you don't have a policy in place for how to handle incorrect shipments, like a way of providing return shipping or how you will make up the delay to the customer, then you will spend more time than you need to scrambling to resolve those complications. Part of being a strong business leader is thinking problems through before they happen. Let's explore what makes a proactive leader.

The Proactive Leader Embraces Change

Being a reactive business manager simply won't work in the long run. You'll be too distracted putting out fires to create the kind of value that builds and grows a business. We've already established that change can be a good thing, and that you need to learn to embrace it, so if you reflected honestly and realized that you are often reacting to challenges, then accept that fact and resolve to evolve into a more proactive leader. Become proactive about your product line, financial state, management challenges, and business. If you see obsolescence of your main product line and don't look for substitutes to stay profitable, then you're not a proactive manager. If you see a competitor surpassing you by offering a lower price on a comparable product, figure out how to reduce costs or how to communicate to your market that your product is worth paying more for. Don't wait until you lose your most loyal customers. Always have contingency plans for cost reduction and marketing in the pipeline so that you're prepared before your hand is forced.

Consider the case of General Motors. GM allowed its car lines to get stodgy and produced something consumers didn't want anymore. It resisted an infiltration of new ideas into the American automobile market and stuck to totally gas-based cars when people were ready for something new. Rather than proactively changing the way GM did business, the company didn't face the harsh reality of its situation and reacted by filing for bankruptcy. On the other hand, there's Apple. Apple evolved its product line even before the obsolescence of existing products. For instance, long before HDMI was the standard, Apple shunned the 25-pin monitor hook-up. It developed firewire before USB proved too slow. Apple didn't cling to the MacBook, but evolved it to other products before phasing it. The company invests heavily in R&D, an incredibly proactive strategy. No matter what your primary widget, if your R&D Department consists primarily of a file folder in the back of your desk drawer, you are not being sufficiently proactive.

The Proactive Leader is Aware of Conditions that Affect His Business

Though it is my intention to stick to advice and topics that transcend technology, industry, economic conditions, and a particular milieu, as I write this book in the midst of one of America's most dramatic economic downturns, I can't help but turn to the economy to address a particular aspect of the proactive CEO. The New Norm, as it's been termed, is the result of the downturn in the economy in the last few years of the first decade of the twenty-first century. Some pundits predicted a flat economy for as many as five-ten years as the United States absorbed a severe decline in real estate value and increases in credit card debt, unemployment, high energy costs, foreclosures and more. As the leader of your company, you must learn to adjust to this New Norm—and any changes in the larger economy—and ask yourself whether or not you're being complacent with business as usual.

To avoid complacency and being lulled into a false sense of security, take concrete steps towards streamlining your business to operate most profitably. Consider fewer fixed assets and more variable ones. For instance, leased or rented assets, instead of purchased ones, can make your business more flexible and prepared for volatile economic conditions. If you can take advantage of competitors' mistakes by acquiring equipment or inventory for twenty cents on the dollar or of the tremendous amount of excess rental, warehouse, and manufacturing space all over the country, a rough economy might be a great opportunity to do so. As you think about these issues, consider your business plan and model. Should it be updated based on the New Norm or the prevailing economic climate? The answer to this isn't always "Yes," but the issue does deserve thoughtful consideration.

The real relevance of addressing the specifics of the New Norm is to emphasize that proactive business leaders are always abreast of the economic, political, and international climate. You may think that those elements don't affect you, but, one way or another, they do. Do you ship anything? Do things move to and from your business—anything at all? If so, stability in the Middle East affects your business. OPEC also affects your business. If you ship, especially with any regularity, any organization, institution, or country that impacts the cost of oil affects your business. Proactive as it would be to own your own supply of natural gas and your own shipping company (though I'm skeptical about whether or not that would pay off in the long run as I can tell you from experience that the oil business is a tough one), the proactive leader need not take such drastic steps. Rather, a proactive CEO not only monitors situations that affect oil but also runs calculations and projections on the potential increases in the cost of shipping; evaluates alternate carriers and shipping methods based on the way they've historically adjusted their prices in response to the price of oil; assesses the attitude of customers and the value they place on faster shipping methods to learn whether or not shipping with slower and less costly services would impact loyalty and satisfaction; and determines the impact of raising the prices of products and services in response to increases in the cost of shipping. That might sound like a lot of work, but being proactive often is. Fortunately, being proactive—in the long term—is always less work than being reactive. Being proactive also keeps you leading your company much longer than being reactive does.

Numerous factors affect your business. Because changes are inevitable, you must stay attuned to them. Take concrete steps to evaluate their impact, while also creating alternative business strategies that mitigate the negative effects any of them might bring.

The Proactive Leader Leads by Example

I can't emphasize this point enough. Whether you are the CEO, owner, president, board member, or manager, you are a leader, and you must lead by example. Poor leadership at any level is poisonous because people follow the example that is set for them, and it doesn't matter whether or not the leader wants people to follow his example—they will. I've seen many a poor example bring down a company. It doesn't matter how many inspiring speeches you give about doing the right thing and behaving a certain way; if your actions don't reflect your words, the latter mean nothing.

My initial turnaround success was a Chapter 11 restructuring at Cheerleader Supply, which was a $65 million a year revenue business with almost 750 employees. As its name suggests, it made cheerleading uniforms, pompoms, and related supplies. Additionally, the company taught cheerleading and directed camps throughout the United States. Cheerleader Supply fell on complicated times and found itself facing a crisis; I was brought in to see it through a Chapter 11 restructuring. What I learned from Cheerleader Supply was why the word "leader" is built right into the cheerleader's position. Cheerleader Supply taught me about the importance of a proactive leader's attitude.

Consider a football game: high school football in Middle America. It's a big deal. Friday at school includes a pep rally, and all afternoon people meander into the school parking lot and stadium. The air is crisp and grows cooler as the evening wears on; by the time Friday night arrives and the game is underway, parents, students, friends, girlfriends, teachers, and other onlookers are cheering enthusiastically from the stands. The first half of the game doesn't go as expected, and people's enthusiasm wanes. Halftime brings a renewed sense of purpose, though, and when the home team comes back out of its locker room everyone is cheering again. Touchdowns don't pick up in the third quarter. The home team is down and everyone's dejected, sitting in his or her seat, hoping for a series of big plays but knowing that they're incredibly unlikely. By the fourth quarter, when its team is down by three touchdowns, the crowd isn't even sure what it's still doing there. The bleachers start to thin. Fortunately, this attitude doesn't beset everyone: Now is the time when cheerleaders truly shine. When the going gets rough—really rough—cheerleaders just cheer harder. They don't sit down. They don't leave. They don't frown. They dance and kick and shout and encourage the entire stadium to get on its feet to give their team the morale, pep, and belief they need to win the game.

Does their team always win because the cheerleaders cheer harder when they're down? Of course not, but you better believe that it's a heck of a lot easier to succeed when people believe you will. And that's what I learned at Cheerleader Supply. As the CEO, it's your job to be the cheerleader for your team, for your company. No matter how low, bad, in debt, damaged, or hopeless the situation gets, it's your job to keep cheering, to keep up the spirit and morale of your team so that it can continue working, fighting, and believing that everything will be okay. It may not always work out in the end, but you have to be the number one force of inspiration. The CEO is a company's head cheerleader, and this attitude, embodied by everyone at Cheerleader Supply, inspired me and allowed me to be the catalyst for change that the company needed. Cheerleader Supply successfully emerged from Chapter 11 bankruptcy.

In a move of slight unprofessionalism that I don't regret even slightly, I gave the judge on our case some Cheerleader Supply pom-poms the day that we emerged from bankruptcy. In fact, I gave everyone in the courtroom that day a set of pom-poms to keep cheering us on during the final come-from-behind score after being so far down in our darkest hour. To this day I still have my own pom-pom in my office. It reminds me of this original successful turnaround the importance of cheering harder, and having the right attitude even when circumstances seem their bleakest. Going forward, I've applied that attitude to every business in which I've been involved. We all lead by example, so make sure yours is a good one.

The Proactive Leader is Not Complacent in Good Times

The great Roman poet, Horace, said, "If matters go badly now, they will not always be so," which is a great characterization of the unavoidable vicissitudes of business. Over the lifetime of a business challenging times are bound to occur. How you prepare as a leader during good times in order to manage during more challenging times is what defines you as a proactive or a reactive leader.

Take Blockbuster, for example. Since its founding in 1985, for nearly two and a half decades business had been going well for the video and gaming rental giant. The company found a combination of products and services that were in high demand, it created a suitable model for distribution, and it grew nationally (and internationally) as a result. You know what happens in this story, though.

> **How you prepare as a leader during good times in order to manage during more challenging times is what defines you as a proactive or a reactive leader.**

Like in most businesses, a competitor came along, a competitor that provided a similar product with a distribution model that cost a fraction of the overhead, a lack of rules regarding rental times and fees, and a method that allowed for an even wider selection. You guessed it: Netflix.

Blockbuster had grown so comfortable with its in-store rental model that it failed to proactively evolve when it had the chance. The rental giant was complacent in good times. Indeed, long after DVDs and digital streaming were the mainstay of movie-watching in America, Blockbuster still allocated large portions of its stores for VHS. Big mistake. The company could argue that people enjoyed visiting a movie store to browse and get recommendations from the local movie jockey, but in an era of online reviews and search-based recommendations, Bobby the Blockbuster stock-boy was no match for Netflix's recommendation algorithm, and by being stuck in the past and lingering there, Blockbuster refused to plan for the future and evolve to cater to the growing consumer base of the digital age. Instead of seeing itself as an entertainment provider, Blockbuster saw itself as a rental facility in a physical space, so they neglected to develop other ways of giving people the entertainment they wanted. And Netflix destroyed them.

In waning years Blockbuster corporate strategists spent most of their time reacting to the evolutions in the movie rental marketplace that Netflix overwhelmingly controlled. They attempted a mailing model that now barely breathes, and when Redbox offered the same service of renting a movie from a physical location but with, again, a fraction of the overhead by creating little movie ATMs, Blockbuster once again reacted by following suit. Blockbuster competes, but at a higher price point, begging the question, what is Blockbuster providing? The answer: not enough. The company filed for Chapter 11 bankruptcy in September 2010. The problem: their reactive leadership got complacent in good times. Blockbuster grew comfortable with what it had accomplished and refused to invest in R&D and experiment in alternative models.

You cannot grow content in good times. Use years of plenty to plan for famine. The funny thing is that those who follow this advice rarely see the latter. Continue to evolve your business no matter your profits. Great businesses do not constantly react to competitors or measure their success by the signposts of others, and they do not rest on their laurels. Instead, they evolve and stay ahead of the curve because their leader is compelled to do so. Blockbuster behaved like an enormous battleship headed along a particular bearing, and that is an incredibly challenging vessel to turn around. Unfortunately for battleships, whether stuck along the same bearing or not, there's none too big to sink. Blockbuster sank. Learn from its mistakes and do not become complacent in good times.

The Proactive Leader is Not a Turtle

The turtle mentality is the staple of a doomed CEO. It involves ducking one's head into his shell to avoid, well, anything. Though turtles with their heads in their shells may be less likely to have their heads bitten off by snapping alligators, they're more likely to miss important opportunities like a good meal or key information about all of the other turtles heading downstream.

The proactive leader never takes the turtle mentality. He never ignores his problems. Instead, he faces them head-on. Larry at the seminar company can be equated to a CEO with the turtle mentality. Whenever there was bad news, he pulled his head into his shell and said, "No!" so that he couldn't hear what that bad news was. He just hoped the alligator would swim on by. The turtle mentality was part of his demise. Keeping your head out of your shell means you're always willing to listen to your employees, and open communication is one of the most important policies a proactive leader can have. People have to feel comfortable coming to you and sharing their concerns about your business.

While acting as the CEO at a company that engaged in twenty-four-hour operations, I knew that we had innumerable problems and that I needed insider information. I decided to host a midnight barbecue for those working the night shift. I brought out a grill and tons of hotdogs and hamburgers with all the fixins' and began grilling and chatting with the team members, jeans on and tie off, trying to learn whatever I could. Seeing me as a regular guy who wanted to hear complaints, swap stories, and hang out over a burger, one of the employees complained about excess inventory purchasing, which after investigation turned out to be a case of multi-million dollar fraud. The employee didn't even know what was happening; he was just sharing something with me that he noticed and that struck him as strange. The CEO preceding me had known that there was something horribly wrong with his company but didn't know what and didn't really want to know. He was faced with a crisis and jammed his head into his shell. In the meantime, I fixed the problem and then had four key executives who were participating in the fraudulent scheme arrested. The CEO disappeared and is believed to be with Jimmy Hoffa, due to some of his underhanded schemes involving the New Jersey unions.

The turtle mentality often plagues the successful CEO as well. After building a business, some CEOs think that they can stow away in their offices, resting on the laurels of their work. You cannot do this. You must walk the floors of your offices, warehouses, factories, and property. You must speak with people; learn what they're doing and why they're doing it. Ask questions. Never stop asking questions. And as important as this is when business is going well, it is crucial during a crisis. No matter how tough your business challenges, as the leader, you have power, influence, and authority, and you cannot be seen ducking into your shell.

The Proactive Leader Never Underestimates Assumptions

Assumptions are part of nearly everything we do and every decision we make, especially in business. The smart business leader recognizes the limitations of all assumptions and predictions. When you learn economics in school or study for an MBA, there's often an elegant simplicity to the scenarios presented and the resultant outcomes, which follow from impractically controlling the environment and isolating variables. Economic theories are challenging to prove because the variables and inputs can't all be controlled or understood, and so the assumptions carry far too much weight. This is often true in business, as well.

Business leaders fail to account for the assumptions they're making and plan for what happens if those assumptions are wrong. The ability to make well-reasoned assumptions in the business world can make you very successful, but the proactive CEO doesn't stake his career on the ability to make the right assumptions. Rather, the proactive CEO ensures that he does not underestimate the power his assumptions have in the first place, and his career is noteworthy for the contingency plans he creates to account for those assumptions.

Jeff Dawkins, the founder of Palm Computing and now a neuroscientist, said, "If you look at the history of big obstacles in understanding our world, there's usually an intuitive assumption underlying them that's wrong." He's right, but unfortunately assumptions are unavoidable, and those who can't make them and move forward are often crippled by inaction. The challenge with assumptions is recognizing when they're made and figuring out how to account for them if they're wrong (and they're often wrong). Accept that assumptions must be made but always question them and make contingency plans to mitigate their effects in case they prove erroneous. When projections are made about the success of a new product line, the effects of an advertising campaign, or the impact on cost structures of certain market changes, demand models and alternatives that account for the assumptions going into those projections being wrong.

I was working with a manufacturing company that had incorrectly forecast how many of a particular widget it was going to be able to sell over the length of its seasonal selling cycle. As a result, this company's CEO found himself sitting on far more merchandise than his line of credit would support and his cash-flow needs would allow. He had made incorrect assumptions. That, however, was not his undoing. Where he failed to be a proactive leader was in not creating a contingency plan for what to do in the event that he ended up with more merchandise than he could sell at a profit, and he was too stubborn to understand that generating any cash out of what he had left was better than sitting on merchandise with little or no current value.

If your business needs cash to survive then it hardly matters how much you can get for non-essential assets like inventory. You need neither flood the market nor destroy the value of your product to generate cash from it. A contingency plan could include a liquidator of your widget, secondhand stores, large outlets like Target and Walmart, a T.J. Maxx or Marshalls, an overseas buyer or any number of other options. Few businesses want to go these routes, but fewer still want to go out of business as an alternative. Proactive leaders ensure that options remain open when assumptions are at play. Had my stubborn CEO had the opposite problem—higher than forecasted demand—he likely would not have had a contingency plan for that either. Imagine the missed opportunity created by faulty assumptions that aren't supported by contingency plans. If only he had prepared factories and warehouses to run twenty-four hours a day for a week straight in case of excess demand, he wouldn't have missed that opportunity either. Wherever there are assumptions, have contingency plans.

The Proactive Leader is Prepared
for Life's Surprises

Life is full of surprises, and as a business leader, you can't let those surprises turn your business upside down. If you learn to manage surprises as part of your business and create contingencies for them—like emergency cash, a fully stocked résumé drawer and interview line for fast hiring, a good network, a solid relationship with your banker, and so forth—then you will survive them.

I was hired to turnaround a small university. After achieving an all-time high enrollment rate and setting the standard of excellence for its under-graduate and masters degree programs, the university was challenged with a loss of accreditation and defaulted on $35 million in secured bond debt. Those are overwhelming problems for an educational institution, and both seemed to come as big surprises to the leaders and board of the university, which is why for me as well as the board and staff, this experience offered a host of lessons about the power of surprises. Upon becoming the director of refinancing and the interim CFO, my partners and I began reworking the budget based on declining attendance and negotiating a forbearance agreement with the bond trustee and its bondholders. Despite this proac-tive approach, there were still surprises for which we had not fully planned.

During our turnaround, the university's CFO had a heart attack and had to undergo bypass surgery. As a key player in the financial situation of the institution, his medical setback gave rise to even greater challenges: we were unable to find all of the documentation we needed to proceed with our turnaround along the projected timeline, to keep the confidence of the bondholders in the integrity of the numbers, and to fully understand the cash flow budget delineated by the CFO. This created tension with the bondholders, a common outcome when a key member of the man-agement team has changed. The CFO wasn't the only key member of the management team we lost. Within six months of the turnaround's start and after less than a year on the job, the president was gone, too. I can't make the case strongly enough that a new president and a new CFO do not breed confidence in lenders. Despite these surprises we continued turning around the university. We pressed forward on the budget, and, despite all odds, successfully renegotiated the forbearance agreement. To keep the institution solvent, we sold some assets and refinanced others while the board searched for a new president.

Though the simultaneity of the president's and CFO's removal was somewhat unique, it represents a common challenge faced by businesses: succession crises. One of the main hurdles bankers face when lending small businesses money is that the entire success of the business revolves around and stops with the owner/founder/CEO/president. This is the hit-by-a-bus problem, and when it occurs, the bank and the heirs/successors face many challenges. That's not because CEOs and buses have a statistically significant bad relationship; it's because bad things happen to people. In the Venn diagram that shows people and CEOs, the CEO circle lies entirely inside of the people circle, so it follows that bad things happen to CEOs. Banks don't want to be at risk of losing their investment based on what could happen to one person. If the CEO is hit by a bus, the bank's investment is gone. Such dramatic events don't even account for the fact that sometimes people just change their minds or lose interest in their business. They also, for example, get left by spouses and become inconsolably depressed, unable to work and fulfill their other obligations.

For these reasons and many others, you need a contingency plan for leadership—a succession plan—to ensure that your business will continue with or without the owner/founder/CEO/president. This increases the likelihood of continued bank support, especially during a crisis. Ensure that the information needed to operate your business is not locked away in your head, and be prepared for a leadership crisis. Write information down in accessible places; have a plan for how someone else could access your computer passwords in the event of an emergency; store contacts in a logical way; groom someone to replace you, whether that replacement is temporary or permanent. Introduce your replacement to bankers and key employees, or, as I've witnessed, crucial team members may jump ship during quagmires or transitions of power. Efforts to delineate the process of transitioning power breed confidence in bankers and investors as well as employees and customers.

Working with the small university also taught me that professionals need to hire consultants and advisors who have different skill sets than their own and that they need to proceed with caution when expanding to areas beyond their core competencies, as the university did when it went into areas beyond its primary mission. The employees at the university were great at their jobs, but they were engaging in business activities that were not their jobs. On some level, this is like the entrepreneur versus professional manager conflict from Chapter 1. The founder with the vision and desire to teach the next generation had to have the entrepreneurial spirit to start the university, but they needed to know when it was time to hire professional business people to handle the overall management of the institution and its finances. All professionals need to understand this salient issue. When professionals venture outside their sweet spots they often make mistakes or don't consider all of the potential challenges and pitfalls. Business is not the forte of all professionals—and it doesn't have to be. Bring in business people to do business. I commend all doctors who are managing successful clinics, but unless you also have business training and experience, you might find the particulars of the operations taxing. You might also find that your time and years of training are better spent healing the sick than balancing budgets and disciplining unruly employees. Hire professionals who can do the work, and prepare your company for the surprises it's bound to face. That's the approach of the proactive leader.

Our work at the university had a happy ending. Within eighteen months, its cash flow was stabilized, accreditation was granted, and the bond debt was refinanced. As part of the long-term plan, the school retained a president and CFO from a competing school. The new president and CFO were monumental in implementing changes necessary to obtain accreditation, including curriculum and core competency. As a true acknowledgment of the victory of this turnaround, our firm, Grisanti, Galef & Goldress, was awarded the Non-profit Turnaround of the Year Award from the Turnaround Management Association (TMA). It turns out that this case was filled with lessons even for other turnaround professionals, central among them that you can't predict what surprises your company will face, but you can still prepare for them.

The Proactive Leader Asks for Help Before It's Too Late

Even the most proactive leader runs into problems that he can't resolve on his own, but the mark of his proactive behavior and self-confidence is that he asks for help before it's too late. Some leaders are challenged to know when they need to ask for professional, outside help. As a general rule of thumb, when you're either panicking or deferring to unqualified people for advice, it's wise to consult an outside professional. Don't worry too much about whether or not you think you don't need help; consultants and turnaround managers with integrity will tell you honestly if you don't need them. I have many meetings with business leaders who invite me in to discuss how I can help them and their businesses. However, our discussions often reveal that they can resolve their problems on their own; these leaders simply needed a pep talk, so I give them as much. Establishing this kind of trust ensures that we will retain open lines of communication, which only further reinforces their proactive approach because I will be on the ready if there is truly a matter that requires my involvement. CEOs who speak early on with me or the other professionals in their networks become confident in their abilities to face their companies' challenges. It is always better to be told that you are okay than to ask for help too late.

I was an advisor for a chain of sports bars in the Midwest. To this day I harbor a lengthy "if only we had" list for that chain, and every last line item is predicated on the fact that had they called us earlier, we could have saved nearly the entire company. Unfortunately, the CEO called us long after the company was in trouble and after filing for bankruptcy without proper planning. In addition, board members self-dealt and worked against us throughout our entire tenure, ultimately revealing cases of fraud and trouble that further hampered our efforts.

If only I had been involved before a large discrimination issue materialized at the sports bar chain, I could have negotiated their crippling predicament and mitigated its demoralizing impact on the team. It takes a professional with experience to do this properly, and your average CEO is too emotional to see clearly the ins and outs of these settlements and negotiations. If only we had arrived when the chain had started experiencing financial crises that constituted an emergency, we would have advised against filing for bankruptcy and salvaged more of the operating business as a result. Under all conditions after we arrived, the chain would have had to file for bankruptcy, but the key to filing is doing so at just the right time—a time when you have created a solid plan, gotten your ducks in a row, and ensured that you are fully aware of all of the challenges that might affect your bankruptcy and emergence. Without that timing, you're doomed. That doesn't mean that we weren't able to help. I did uncover one of my best fraud stories at the sports bar chain that would likely have remained undetected otherwise, and that created value for the chain. (See Chapter 5.) Learn from this company's mistake and ask for help before it's too late.

A CEO at another company asked for help before it was too late, and that made all the difference. I was brought in to consult on a company that had just purchased another company from another state. Absorbing competitors who could broaden their market share and offerings was part of this company's business plan, but what they lacked was a concrete way of making this happen. In this case, the purchasing company was in Florida, and the company it was buying was in Minnesota. Neither of these was a small company, and yet the management team in Orlando, FL believed that it was going to shut down operations in Minnesota on a Thursday evening and move them to Florida over the course of a long weekend so that they'd be up and fully operational by Monday.

My jaw dropped when I heard this plan, because, well, it was not a plan. It was a fantasy. Not only was it a sheer impossibility to pack up all of the unique manufacturing equipment in Minnesota, load it onto trucks and drive it to Florida where it had to be unloaded and reassembled properly in a weekend, but no one in Florida knew how to screw the parts together or operate this equipment come Monday. There was also no one to train the Orlando workers or even a physical space in which to place this newly assembled equipment. The "plan" was asinine: the least planning I'd ever seen. The good news is that the leadership team brought me in early enough, and we were able to prepare adequately and before they lost inordinate sums of money; this involved confronting the reality of their goals, creating realistic expectations, communicating with all key team members, building a timeline with contingency plans, and getting buy-in from everyone involved. The preparation was essential and the move was successful. Had they waited to bring me in until after an unsuccessful move, they would have had a true crisis on their hands. In this case, all they had was a business consultant and a successful move. What a difference that was from my experience at the sports bar chain.

The Proactive Leader Does Not Get Shot At

I have been shot at twice. I am sometimes shot at because I clean up the messes of non-proactive leaders, and as the perceived proxy of the non-proactive leader, people like to aim at me.

I was the chief restructuring officer of a company we'll call Big Steel. We were in a staff meeting debating the effects of imported Asian steel on our cost structure (for the record, the effects were bad, very bad), and we decided that in order to remain competitive we needed to reduce our 2,500-person workforce by at least 10 percent while also reducing union employee benefits. The day before we'd discussed this demoralizing reduction with the union representative, and though nothing was official, the news was out. As you now know, your employees always know.

BAM!! BAM!! BAM!! BAM!!

All of a sudden four shotgun blasts smashed into the windows.

I hit the floor.

Astonishingly, I was the only one to duck, and the other senior staff started laughing at me. In one of the most simultaneously reactive and proactive moves of all time, they'd installed bulletproof windows in the boardroom twenty years prior because shotgun blasts from the union were not an uncommon event. They were just the employees' way of showing dissatisfaction. No big deal, right?

So why did we really get shot at? You may say, loose gun laws in the workplace, but if shotgun blasts had been fired at the boardroom for the last twenty years, then obviously there was something else wrong at Big Steel.

This manufacturing company was facing a crisis caused by a multitude of factors, including a significant investment in manufacturing equipment, a reliance on older technology, and a huge cash crisis resulting from a stronger, lower-cost competitor. At this stage, our only option to contain costs was a reduction in the workforce, which was tragic for 250 people and their families. However, if the CEO had been proactive in keeping costs down six to twelve months prior, these kinds of dramatic and last-minute cost reduction options could have been implemented more gradually and reasonably—and in ways that didn't affect the union so dramatically. The company did take some proactive measures by seeking help from the US government for dumping and was involved in litigation. But these measures weren't enough and eighteen months after the new CEO was hired, the company was liquidated. You, as a business leader, must be aware of ongoing activity in your marketplace and competitive space and take early steps to mitigate any negative effects on your business.

Suddenly having to fire a tenth of a workforce and reduce benefits in a desperate measure to stay afloat are the signs and results of reactive leadership. When your market share is decreasing due to strong competition, you execute a previously developed austerity program while figuring out how to compete under the new conditions. And then you don't get shot at. For the record, however proactive I consider myself to be and however bulletproof the glass, when I hear unexpected shotgun blasts, I hit the deck. Just call it my bulletproof glass contingency plan.

The Proactive Leader Leverages His Current Business Plan and Prepares and Develops Contingency Plans

Sun Tzu, the revered Chinese military general, philosopher and strategist, spoke at length about the value of preparation, and contended that he wouldn't voluntarily engage in battle without preparations that already assured him of victory before the battle began. Since Sun Tzu has influenced generals and CEOs for centuries, long before the turnaround profession existed, I'll throw his clout behind this assertion about proactive leaders.

The initial preparation-based document of most businesses is the business plan. You know, that document that your angel investor/banker/ spouse/partner/parents wanted to see to make sure that you weren't totally out of your mind when you told them you were going to start a business? The point of that document was, in part, to prepare you for many of the issues that would inevitably arise over the course of doing business—to force you to think them through. Do you need special permits or authorization? How much will your operating expenses be the first five years? When do you expect to turn a profit and what will your subsequent growth rate look like? What are your competitors' barriers to entry or can anyone hijack your idea? These preparatory questions by no means guarantee success, but they are certainly steps in the right direction, since without answering them, you are far more likely to fail or face the sorts of challenges that cripple you, your time, and your company.

One of the first documents a leader refers to in questionable times is his business plan. Your company was created with a purpose, a goal, a higher calling. You initially researched problems, competitors, products, investors, markets, capitalization, and so much more. You were cross-examined by those around you, and you took extra time to ensure that you were headed down the right path. If you did any of your business planning conventionally, you put all of your thoughts and answers to these questions into a

> **How you prepare as a leader during good times in order to manage during more challenging times is what defines you as a proactive or a reactive leader.**

well thought out and neatly bound document. In a crisis, turn to it. You never know what advice it may hold in terms of predicting these problems, methods of resolving them, or unique directions to take the business given the opportunity.

Leveraging your business plan also means keeping it updated. The truly engaged CEO is morphing his company's business plan as his business changes. Businesses and the business environment are always transforming, and it is essential that your business plan keep pace with those changes. Learn from proactive leaders who leverage their business plans, business plans that have kept up with them and their companies. If it's been ten years since you began your business—or fifty years—then your business plan may be dated. Technology, leadership, and impromptu opportunities may have led your business in unforeseen directions. Don't wait until you're experiencing a crisis to update your business plan and think through contingencies. Open that document and start modifying it based on current facts and financial realities. While business is going well, don't get complacent. Think through the many kinds of crises I've been discussing and update your business plan to address what you'd do in the event that any of them happened to you or your business. It is never too soon to think these challenges through and develop contingency plans. This is how you prepare your company to grow in good times and weather the storm in bad periods.

So what should one think about in terms of contingency plans? An easy place to start is your banking relationship. Cash is, after all, the lifeblood of any business. Without proper cash flow you won't be able to buy inventory, make payroll, or pay your bills. Do you have a line of credit? If so, is it in use? Could you stand to ask for it to be expanded while times are good and your banker is predisposed? Do you have good relationships with multiple banks? There are hundreds of banks across the country that are failing but can't be taken over by the FDIC because the FDIC lacks the resources to pick up the pieces of all failed banks. That should make you nervous if you're banking at any of these less stable institutions, and it should also set you on a quest for banking contingency plans. Find multiple banks with whom to do business. The flip side of the coin is that banks can lose confidence in those they've funded or lent money to, and in the event that this happens you don't want to be scrambling to find another bank—especially in times of tighter credit. Bank relationships are best developed when business is going well, so ensure you have a backup bank.

Speaking of quick cash needs, consider the assets you might liquidate in case of an emergency. Is there anything non-essential that would fetch a fair value? Do you know who would buy it? I'm not suggesting you sell assets early. I'm only suggesting that you know what you would liquidate and how if you had to do so. Alternatively, rather than liquidating assets, consider how you might raise additional capital or perhaps sell or merge your business.

These are the questions that a proactive leader considers long before he's confronted with the harsh reality of their actuality—and often the CEO who knows the answers to these questions is the kind of leader whose reality never gets harsh enough for these plans to matter.

We've already reviewed the importance of a good succession plan, and I'll trust that you stopped reading long enough to put your succession plan in motion—and in writing. So once you've thought about your role and who would succeed you as CEO, you must consider the other key positions at your company. Who is indispensable to your operations? What would you do if something happened to him or her? How would you replace that person? Think about your network and the resources available to you should you need to replace a key member of your team quickly. Who else at your company knows how that person does his or her job? More importantly, if someone disappeared and had to be replaced, could you or someone else show a new person how to do the job in question? CEOs often imagine that employees will be around to train those who replace them, but they don't confront the reality that someone might leave under more sudden circumstances (like the university's CFO). There should be extensive documentation about what every position in your company does, what's expected of the person occupying that position, and what she or he needs to access and know. Require a detailed write-up from everyone.

Consider your industry and the kinds of emergencies that it usually faces. Is it a highly regulated industry? Is it litigious? Are your products safety related? What could go horribly wrong in your industry and business? Think about these potential challenges and use your core team to brainstorm solutions in case any emergency hits. Don't ever be left wondering what you're going to do in the event of a crisis.

Over the course of the last decade, there has been an increasing concern in our country about the outbreak and sudden spread of some kind of pandemic flu. With the scares over bird flu and H1N1, the US government used key resources to develop an intensive and thorough contingency plan for what we would do if a highly contagious and crippling flu swept across North America. Corporate partners with drive-throughs like national pharmacy chains and fast-food restaurants were recruited to be distribution centers where supplies and medicines would be handed out without people having to come into close contact with one another; plans for continuing education from home without children contaminating each other at school were developed. While some of the more extreme elements of this plan have not yet been implemented, certain less dramatic aspects were executed during the outbreak of H1N1, and these measures helped diminish the impact of the flu. This was possible because the government used key members of the CDC under the Department of Health and Human Services to create such a contingency plan. Hopefully, we will never need it, but it's there nonetheless. That was a proactive move by an organization that took steps to plan before a crisis emerged.

Some allege that having contingency plans implies that you don't believe in your primary business plan and are therefore destined to failure. That is naive and shortsighted. Every proactive general believes his plan of attack will work or else he wouldn't try it, but I assure you that if he's worthy of his position he has a plan B and knows the best method of retreat (consult Sun Tzu's *The Art of War* for more). Having a viable backup plan doesn't undermine a good leader's initial success. It bolsters his confidence and that of his men, ensuring a greater likelihood of success and survival. That is the essence of optimism bolstered by realism that we discussed towards the end of Chapter 2. Rely confidently on a well thought-out business plan, but be realistic and ensure you have appropriate contingency plans. Don't think of contingency plans as something extra—they are part of the main plan. There are assumptions built into every plan, and since assumptions and projections are often wrong, prepare extensively.

Chapter 4

Danger Signs and Dollar Signs: Make Your Banker Your Partner

Cash is the lifeblood of every business. It is not, however, the purpose of every business. If you think that money is the central purpose of your business then I highly suggest you reevaluate what you're trying to accomplish. That said, you can't have a business without cash. While bootstrapping is a commendable effort and certainly possible, at various stages of a business's life, larger amounts of capital are required to grow or survive. Whether to purchase a warehouse or equipment, make significant hires, or just to have a line of credit for inevitabilities, CEOs need banks and bankers, which is to say, their money. Cultivating a good relationship with your banker is not only essential to getting the financing you need now but also to keeping it when times are more challenging.

Many CEOs and presidents see their bankers as the opposition and as people whom they have to challenge and beguile, manipulate, or even act obsequiously towards. That's just not so. Your banker is and should be your ally—not your adversary. People do get crazy about money, and I've known many a banker to knee-jerk about funds he thought were at risk—remember, I was once a banker, too—so respect your banker and his needs.

The easiest way to turn bankers into adversaries is by lying to them and withholding essential information. Bankers find deception unforgivable and they love to be informed; yet CEOs have a habit of keeping them in the dark. Let's rethink our banking relationships to create better long-term results.

The 10 C's of Bank Relationships for CEOs

Through my 10 C's of Bank Relationships you can better understand your banker, what he thinks about, and how to have a fruitful and affable relationship with him. I've developed these guidelines because bankers and business owners often have trouble communicating due to their differing mindsets. As a former banker with thirty years of interim CEO experience, I have harmonized an understanding of the banker's approach with the knowledge of what makes businesses run successfully from the top. Learn from the mistakes of CEOs who failed to understand their bankers and suffered as a result by recognizing that you're in a partnership with your banker. He wants you to be successful: it's the only way you both get paid. These 10 C's of Bank Relationships for CEOs should help you become a better borrower, enhance your relationship with your banker and make money more available when your business needs it most.

1. Character

Character is of utmost importance to bankers. Bankers need to know you'll do the right thing when your company is in distress. If they can't trust you, they can't put money in your hands. That doesn't mean fake good character—it means have and demonstrate good character.

I stepped in once at a small manufacturing company where the charming and charismatic owner had managed to acquire substantial loans from his banks. I was brought in because the owner also managed to squander those loans in a series of inept moves. The banker kept telling me that the owner had seemed to have such good character, to be so trustworthy, but the banker felt he had been duped.

My job negotiating with a bank is considerably easier when the owner of a company has demonstrated good character in the past. This good character keeps the banker's fears at bay and inclines him to work with, rather than against, the business owner.

2. Carelessness

Carelessness in business is directly related to poor recordkeeping. It is only with good records that you can prove your credit-worthiness and trustworthiness to your banker and others evaluating your business. Running your shop well includes good bookkeeping practices, regular audits, competent controllers, and mixing up your monitoring practices. Continually verify reports of your business's financial situation. Demonstrate the care you do take in all operational aspects of your business, and you will strengthen your banking relationships.

3. Complacency

Where carelessness will turn your banker off, complacency will anger him. Banks are interested in how you react to tough situations and fear complacency because it indicates that you will not communicate clearly and often. Don't just tell bankers what you're legally required to when they ask; keep them updated to avoid surprises. We talked about the surprises that face businesses and their leaders, and I want to assure you that you have an ally in your distaste for those surprises: your banker. Proactive business owners keep their bankers apprised. The bankers are then less likely to react to unfortunate circumstances by demanding an immediate repayment of loans, which you'll note below many of them have a right to do.

At the sports bar chain, the CEO and board were complacent; they did not proactively share with their bank the challenges they were having, and as a result, their banker put an enormous amount of pressure on them and created deadlines that could not be met. On the other hand, at the small university, when the CFO had a heart attack and we terminated our president, I immediately disclosed this situation to the bondholders and other creditors. Though I knew that this would not breed confidence, they had to hear it from me directly. Otherwise, I would never have had a chance of convincing them that I could handle the situation.

Complacency has consequences other than disappointed bankers. It causes companies to be less competitive and neglect an assessment of their costs. Complacent CEOs find themselves selling products below cost, as they do not update their manufacturing cost analyses on a regular basis. I had an electronic manufacturer with massive losses because the sales manager was discounting product to move it, and no one was evaluating the costs often enough to catch this. Coupled with an already inaccurate MRP system, this negligent error almost sunk the company. The owner had to make a tough choice: infuse cash to save the company or let the business go under. He needed to perform a huge reanalysis of his business costs and margins because of inaccurate controls and cost accounting, but he did not. He was complacent. Had he been sufficiently proactive, this analysis would have been happening all the while, and he could have taken control sooner and lost less money. Instead, the lack of growth and confidence pushed the banker to react strongly, and the company was sold off in pieces.

4. Contingency Plans

We reviewed contingency plans in Chapter 3; now, count contingency plans among your 10 C's of Bank Relationships.

Bankers value stability, and even though many business owners think they're invincible, history has proven otherwise. If your bank knows what will happen in the event that something bad happens to you—the 3 D's, disability, disappearance (I've had a couple of CEOs vanish), or death—they will be comforted. If they know what will happen to your business in the event of a catastrophe because you've already outlined a series of contingency plans, they'll continue to work with you or subsequent leadership. It's also wise to introduce your banker to your potential replacement.

Joe was 100 percent owner and guarantor on a distribution business loan. He developed cancer, which took his life two years later. Mary, his wife, ran the business during his final two years, and after Joe's funeral, the banker called the loan because the guarantor was dead. Had Joe introduced his wife to the banker, he would have seen that she was running and could run the business's operations, and it wouldn't have taken us ninety days to convince the banker that Mary knew the company, could be a guarantor, and that the company could and should survive.

5. Capital

Capital is your net worth (assets minus liabilities). Bankers are delighted to see a lot of capital because it means that you have a fiscal cushion and that they are more likely to be repaid regularly and in a timely fashion. However, during a crisis the cushion normally disappears, so bankers want an extra chunk of equity. That way, they can be more flexible with your company in case it has a bad year (i.e., a negative number on your year-end P&L). Ensure that you always have the capital you need to remain fiscally solvent by properly saving money when business is going well. Every dollar earned can't be reinvested in the business or paid out. It's important that the business has capital reserved for emergencies or leaner years. That's right: banks like to see savings. If banks see that you recognize the importance of savings, they will be more likely to work with you.

6. Collateral

Collateral is a bank's leverage. In addition to capital, collateral makes bankers feel more comfortable. Collateral does not repay a loan, as many entrepreneurs think when they pledge their assets, but collateral is a secondary source of repayment because it can be liquidated. Easing your banker's mental burden manages your banking relationship. Bankers want as much collateral as they can get to ensure their investment and minimize risk. Treat collateral as an opportunity to demonstrate your honest intentions and confidence in your business plan and contingency plans. It's worth noting that in any turnaround, bankers want additional collateral and more guarantees. If you can avoid giving up everything during normal times, you'll have something left to bargain a forbearance or renewal in the event of the unfortunate.

7. Capacity

Capacity is your ability to repay. While it certainly takes into account some of the factors mentioned above, there's more finesse to this one. Bankers check to see if you have champagne tastes but a beer wallet. Are you frivolous? Do you love the biggest, brightest, and best? Do you have a history of being attracted to shiny objects? Of course all of these tastes and predilections are permissible, but your banker is going to wonder why you're asking for money for essential elements of your operation while simultaneously buying new equipment where used would have worked just as well—and Rolexes, airplanes, and Ferraris. Corporate airplanes and high-life cars are often danger signs to bankers.

At the first financial speed bump, guess what goes first: the possibility of a loan because you're not seen as having the capacity needed to repay. On the contrary, if you seem like you can repay what you're asking for—which is to say, a reasonable sum and not your dream loan—you're more likely to see the money. Shoot for the stars in life, but a bank loan is a different matter. Ask for what you need and for what you know you can repay. Bankers like people who are down to earth and reasonable. They're easier to work with and more likely to repay. Remember, a loan isn't just money: there's a relationship behind it, and you have to learn how to manage that relationship and its accompanying expectations.

8. Competition

Competition works to your advantage, at least in this aspect of your business. Usually, you're working to overcome your competition, but when it comes to your banking relationships, you want to leverage the existence of banking competition for your benefit. Banks are concerned about their competitors' interest rates, collateral packages, and guarantees. By doing your homework when seeking a loan and illuminating your understanding of the landscape to your banker, you convey to him that you are serious about working hard in the best interest of your business while simultaneously informing him that he's not the only banker on the block.

Be careful when proffering competitors' details, though, as no one likes to feel threatened with, "If I don't get exactly what I want here I'll go elsewhere." Instead, tactfully use the element of bank competition to negotiate for more competitive rates, less collateral, and extended terms. Perhaps figure out how to reduce or eliminate that personal guarantee. Knowing and staying informed about your bank's competition can also let you prepare for a quick capital search should your banker pull out of your arrangement. Turn the competition among banks to your advantage by cultivating multiple bank relationships.

9. Controls

Controls are your built-in monitors at your business, and they will be discussed extensively in Chapter 5. Controls, like inventory counts, two signees for checks, etc., are one of the 10 C's of Bank Relationships because of the important role they play in your banker's perception of your business's management. Bankers want to know all about your company's controls, and they want to be kept regularly apprised of updates to those controls. Do you have checks and balances for payroll clerks, controllers, CFOs, and inventory? Do you watch the back door? With what? Cameras? Rottweilers? Do you review your books? Do you have superstar auditors?

During your conversations with bankers, it pays to outline the preventative, regulatory, and review measures you have implemented or plan to introduce in your business. Solicit recommendations about your fraud policy from your banker, CPA, and financial advisor. CPAs and accountants who have been in the business world a while have seen their fair share of failed businesses, some of which went under due to fraudulent activity or a lack of controls. Many accountants are bound to have some useful general suggestions or even particular advice related to your business. The fact that you have an open conversation with your banker about the topic demonstrates that you are aware of the related challenges. Moreover, it deepens your credibility, is a sign of good character, debunks concerns that you're lazy, and incentivizes him to have a relationship with you.

What can you do if you uncover an issue that skirted your controls, particularly any kind of fraudulent activity? Always fix the problem first, and then update your banker on your resolution process and the steps you are taking to prevent the same mistake from happening in the future. Of course he'll be concerned about the notion that money was stolen or that controls failed, but your open communication, results-oriented attitude, and problem solving will reassure him.

10. Communication

Communication is essential, and almost every one of the 10 C's hinges on communication. Nothing is more important to a banker than good communication, especially considering how many clients and businesses keep him in the dark because they're scared of what he'll do or because they don't think he needs to know. When you were 17 you knew that you had to tell your parents when you dinged the fender on their car even though they'd be upset. At the same time, you knew that by telling them what had happened you'd be solidifying their trust for the future because they could expect that you'd be honest about other problems. Not communicating honestly with your banker is the wrong approach and one of the quickest ways to have your loan called or to lose your financing. Don't keep things from your banker. If he knows what's happening, he can work with you instead of against you.

A Case Study in the 10 C's of Bank Relationships for CEOs

Most turnarounds illustrate only a few of the 10 C's of Bank Relationships for CEOs, but one notable case—that of a company we'll call Giant Manufacturing in the Southwest—includes so many of the 10 C's that I want to share it with you as a cautionary tale. The troubles of this manufacturer surfaced in 2007, and a proactive CEO would have been aware of their inevitability well before they became a full-blown crisis. For decades prior to 2007, business was booming for Giant Manufacturing, but after many years of profitability, and coinciding with the broader economic decline in the United States, unprofitable long-term contracts with major customers resulted in severe declines in cash flow and ultimately the business overall. The lack of awareness of unprofitable contracts is a prime example of Complacency; no one had taken the time when business was good to maintain profitability evaluations on large (and small) contracts. The company failed to notify the bank in a timely and effective fashion of the major losses that it was suffering, and you know that this lack of Communication about their capacity displeased the bank.

Our firm's involvement was precipitated by the anxiety of the bank about the alarming trends related to profitability, contracts, and cash flow. As we already know, bankers hate surprises, and considering the size of this client, the surprise was overwhelming enough that they opted to cut back on Giant Manufacturing's availability, which means shrinking the cash available for the company to operate by decreasing the amount the company could borrow against its receivables. When we arrived at Giant Manufacturing, we were asked to act as advisors to find new financing opportunities because the bank no longer wanted to support this unstable giant. Most sources had already declined to fund the company, and unfortunately Giant Manufacturing's CEO had not been sufficiently proactive to cultivate multiple bank relationships before we arrived. That could have averted part of this crisis. Other aspects of our engagement included streamlining operations and renegotiating contracts more profitably while acting as interim CFO. We were given a six-month forbearance to create a miracle or the company would be liquidated.

Our major challenges extended beyond the unprofitable contracts and unfavorable cost structure that resulted from prior carelessness and poor accounting and record keeping; we learned that the company was operating in a saturated and highly competitive market, and so it therefore had limited ability to raise prices despite improved operations. That is, if customers wanted to go to another supplier they could find comparable services at potentially better rates with little trouble. Unfortunately, Giant Manufacturing had no Contingency Plan for this kind of problem. Had there been other services or benefits to doing business with them in the pipeline it would have been easier to retain customers despite raised prices.

We began where we had to: renegotiating long-term distribution contracts that were generating losses. I highly recommend that you regularly assess your contracts to ensure that none of them have you locked into losses. If they do, extricate yourself from those contracts or renegotiate them so that both you and your clients/customers are benefiting fairly. I don't believe in loss leaders, and I rid a company of any I find. You won't last long with detrimental contracts. In addition, we reengineered the cost structure to accommodate prevailing economic conditions. We worked with the company leadership to eliminate unprofitable product lines, renegotiate vendor debt, and execute on a forbearance agreement with the senior lender. We also solidified a long-term contract with a key customer, which increased the top line enough to demonstrate that we would have the Capital needed to run the operation profitably.

> **I highly recommend that you regularly assess your contracts to ensure that none of them have you locked into losses.**

Implementing tighter credit criteria was also a must. We had to make sure that more customers—especially the less stable ones—were either better vetted or required to put a deposit on their accounts. That would insulate us for at least 30-60 days in the event that too high a percentage of customers failed to pay their bills. Consider your credit risk based on your customer base, and overhaul your system to reduce your risk. We also shortened the payment terms for all of Giant Manufacturing's customers and instituted tighter payment criteria.

Laying off staff was necessary, as well. It's important to remember that even though layoffs are a tough order to execute, letting some workers go saves the jobs of many others by saving the company overall. Learn from the mistakes of past CEOs who went through layoff after layoff, decimating the morale of their companies. If you must let people go, do so in one confident move. If you have multiple layoffs weeks or even months apart, you will demoralize your employees by making them feel insecure in their positions. Though most of our efforts with Giant Manufacturing were geared towards leaner operations, the above steps ensured the company's immediate survival. Over the course of sixteen months, Giant Manufacturing shifted from losing significant amounts of money to having a positive cash flow position. It returned to profitability, and a new two-year bank loan was executed with a new lender. Due to the speed of the turnaround, the new lender elected to extend Giant Manufacturing's credit, which was a welcome bonus and the bank's way of saying that we had re-infused confidence and trust into the relationship.

An important factor in our healthy partnership with the new bank was that we educated our prospective banker about our turnaround efforts and successes (as well as our challenges). Do not underestimate the importance of Communication as a crucial element in this overall case. As of the writing of this book, the company has an excellent relationship with its bank that includes ongoing and honest communication. In fact, the company completed an acquisition in 2011, and its employees received raises across the board because of the respectable Character their leadership demonstrated.

Consider the facts that your banker will find important: if your company is highly leveraged, has a decreasing cash cushion, and is maxed out on its credit, it's time to take more serious action. Your banker begins by behaving with a mind towards your success, but you have to make his life easier, and that means following the 10 C's of Bank Relationships for CEOs. Your bank relationship is one of the most important ones in your business, a fact that will be thrown into sharp relief should you ever face a crisis. Make sure that you make every effort—especially while your business is healthy—to communicate with your banker and to understand him, so that you are always working with rather than against him.

The Rotten Ratio

Every industry and business has interesting ratios and rates that are relevant to it. In my business, we have a ratio that I call the Rotten Ratio. The Rotten Ratio is when sales equals debt. Take a second to think about that: sales equals debt. Believe it or not, I see a number of companies in this situation, which begs the question, how does something like that happen? Why do I keep getting hired at this rotten spot?

When business is good and sales are increasing, companies buy a new factory or purchase new equipment. To do this, they borrow money, which at the time makes sense when they look at their sales and growth. However, as tends to happen, especially when companies and their leaders get distracted, sales slow down, yet that debt is still there. Numerous warning signs should likely have tipped off CEOs, owners, and boards to the tsunami headed their way, but we already know how many CEOs make the mistake of not seeking professional help early enough.

A worldwide swimwear manufacturer spent a pleasantly long time enjoying increasing sales. To keep up with its growth, it built several manufacturing plants, hired more employees, and bought more raw materials. The company was growing and making money fast. At some point, though, sales started declining because its designs were either not socially acceptable or not forward thinking enough in the markets to which it was selling. What happened to this company is what happens to so many manufacturers. It was riding a wave, and the wave leveled off. Instead of keeping its costs variable, it had ended up with numerous fixed costs—a classic mistake—and the borrowed money for all of those fixed costs in tandem with the declining sales ultimately resulted in the meeting of debt and sales.

The only way a company can survive this ugly ratio is with a lot of luck, an understanding of bankers and creditors, and proof to the aforementioned that they're better off alive than dead. Nurture those three things and not only might you weather this classic ratio, but you will probably avoid it in the first place.

Self-Dealing:
How to Undermine Your Bank Relationships

Nothing hinders a turnaround like officers or owners working against their creditors, and me, by self-dealing. One example of self-dealing is when an officer of a company tries to gain an unfair tactical advantage, by "understating profits" and attempting to purchase the company, for example. Self-dealing is not necessarily stealing, but it is fraudulent if not properly disclosed to all parties. In short, when a company is insolvent, legally, the fiduciary responsibilities of the officers and directors of that company shift from a duty to the shareholders to a duty to the creditors. When I'm brought into a company, insolvency is at the very least either already roosting or cresting the horizon, so if any officer is creating value for himself or the shareholders instead of the creditors, this is automatically considered self-dealing.

In one huge turnaround case, I was blindsided by an officer of the company who was trying to buy the assets of the business through a shell company. He obviously wasn't acting in the best interests of the creditors because he was trying to drive down the price of assets to purchase them himself. With proper disclosure to the creditors and without other credible purchasers in the game, the creditors could approve what would otherwise be self-dealing, but it's a fine line that requires honesty and communication. By creating a process that inserts a turnaround manager in the company, self-dealing is far less likely to occur, or in the event that it does, it will be revealed, like in the case of this shell company. Though I'd had an early gut feeling that someone was self-dealing, I wasn't able to expose what was happening before I had to speak with the creditors. Therefore, despite my promising the creditors that there was no self-dealing, an officer was doing exactly that, and he made me look foolish. The revelation of his actions undermined my credibility with the creditors and created a conflict between the officer and me, which delayed the resolution of the case. Minimize risk and damage to yourself and the company by keeping your intentions honest and communicating your actions to all parties involved.

In this particular case I was required to give expert testimony, and when I testify I have to know the truth; I pride myself on my ability to uncover the truth when I'm working a case. If you don't trust someone in your operation, as the leader, you must keep an eye on him. Ask lots of questions. Many CEOs make the mistake of feeling guilty about mistrust. This serious error can cost a leader his business. If the person you do not trust does nothing wrong then you will find nothing wrong in the long run and be pleased. Better to make that mistake than the opposite, which is to ignore your gut feelings and fail to protect yourself, your business and its interests. In your business, you have to be able to ask whatever you need of whomever you need without feeling guilty or uncomfortable. Your banker and other creditors likely don't know others in your business besides you. They know you, and they need to be able to trust you, something they can do only if you have shown them that you can be the regulator of truth at your business.

The Power of Bank Documents

It never fails to amaze me that most of my clients sign bank documents, stick them in the drawer, and don't look at them until years later when there are problems and someone is invoking a clause that will cause them to lose everything for which they've worked. Every CEO should reread his bank documents on an annual basis so that he understands and reminds himself of the collateral, financial covenants, and limitations to which he's signed his name (limitations include stipulations like the owner's compensation or change of control provisions that could inadvertently trip up an otherwise sound banking relationship). Create PDFs of your documents and keep them on your computer or tablet so that you can review them on an airplane or even at the beach. I don't care where you reread them—just read them annually.

One CEO I rescued was in the business of importing tulips. He assumed that a piece of property he owned—a cold storage distribution center that he had financed five years prior—was free and clear of all debt. Contrary to this assumption, the bank did not release the lien on this loan when it was paid in full but had the cold storage distribution center as side collateral. The CEO failed to recall that the bank retained the warehouse as additional collateral on his initial large line of credit. He mistakenly thought he could get a quick loan on the building, create some interim cash, and get through a crunch. The bank declined this proposal because the storage facility was already collateral, so the CEO and his tulip company had no immediate way of resolving their cash crisis. Had he regularly reviewed his documents, his memory would have served him better, and he would have created a different contingency plan for any credit crunch.

Another CEO who was in the furniture manufacturing business was financed by both SBA and another bank. Apparently, though, it slipped his mind that his total compensation in any given year could not exceed $100,000. This was a stipulation of the SBA loan, which guaranteed 90 percent of the bank's loan. In order to keep that 90 percent guarantee, however, the bank had to be sure to immediately enforce every nuance of the original loan. Thus, as soon as the bank learned that the owner was paid several multiples of his $100,000 salary cap in a single calendar year, it defaulted on his loan. Since he could not repay the loan and recapitalize the company, this furniture manufacturer had to be liquidated so that the banker received his SBA guaranteed loan. If the CEO had wanted more money, he could have renegotiated his loan in good times with the SBA's approval or obtained a waver in a specific year. However, because he didn't regularly review the terms of his loan and he didn't communicate with his banker, he violated those terms and lost everything.

Then there was Tom. Tom had a steel fabricating business in Texas, and as part of his bank documents for his business's line of credit there was a change of control provision. Normally, a change of control provision relates to selling 51 percent of a business. That is, if someone is selling more than half of his business, he is required to consult the bank first, who often reserves some right of refusal. However, Tom was in need of cash and wanted to expand. Due to a few operating losses he sold 40 percent of his business to an investor group, thinking that wouldn't violate his agreement. The change of control definition in his long-standing bank document was that he needed the bank's approval if he did not retain a super majority, or 67 percent ownership (as opposed to the more standard 51 percent). The banker had a bad experience with Tom's investor on another private deal and out of concern he called Tom's loan, which of course Tom didn't have the cash to repay. He was then forced to sell the remainder of his company to this investor group for pennies on the dollar in order to protect himself from the personal guarantee on the bank loan. All of this happened because Tom didn't regularly reread his bank documents, nor did he communicate with his banker before a transaction out of the normal scope of operations.

Reviewing your bank documents annually isn't the only aspect of contracts that should have your attention. It's exceedingly important that when signing loan documents you only sign a personal guarantee for a specific transaction. This is contrary to what bankers require, but that shouldn't stop you from letting these documents get the better of you. Bankers normally require a personal guarantee that is evergreen, meaning that it applies for the transaction at hand as well as any future transactions or loans. That is, your personal guarantees always apply. Do not sign evergreen personal guarantees. Keep each personal guarantee limited to a specific transaction.

In 1994 Walter and Joe started a distribution business in Atlanta, and they personally guaranteed certain vendor shipments as well as a $100,000 loan from their bank. Ten years later, after rapid growth and the accompanying increase in accounts payable and bank loans, they owed the bank several million dollars—this alongside a precipitous rise in vendor obligations. By 2007 the company started having severe financial problems and considered filing for reorganization under a bankruptcy. As you can imagine, though, one of the first actions I take at a new company is reading bank documents, and I learned that Walter and Joe guaranteed everything they had on loan in 2007 with their original 1994 loan documents. They had believed that their original personal guarantees were limited to $100,000 on their original loans and therefore no longer existed. They were wrong, and they were on the hook for millions. Generally, banks get everything signed anew for fresh loans, including a personal guarantee. This old country bank just didn't do it that way, so Walter and Joe had been personally guaranteeing everything for the last thirteen years and didn't remember signing those documents. Similarly, the guarantee covered millions of dollars of vendor debt. We had to reconsider the bankruptcy option because the personal guarantees would have required them to file personal bankruptcies as well, and they would have lost everything. As an alternative, after many months we sold the company by negotiating a short payment to the bank, and the new owners maintained the vendors' cooperation. Learn from the mistakes of ruined CEOs and refuse to sign evergreen clauses in your loan documents.

Most bank documents have certain financial covenants. The basic one is a simple debt coverage ratio. That means that the company must produce cash flow in excess of the debt service. Usually this ratio is 1.25:1. That means, for example, that if you're paying a bank $100,000 a year in interest payments they want to make sure that your EBITDA is in excess of $125,000 because it gives the bank a cushion and comfort, allowing them to react more quickly if cash flow issues present themselves. Any business that has negative earnings or negative cash flow automatically fails this ratio because the numerator is negative. I've seen this ratio trip up hundreds of companies and destroy their bank relationships. The reason is not the ratio itself, which is entirely reasonable, but that most CEOs don't build in a "cure period" that allows them to get the ratio back in line before the bank is allowed to interfere. Most banks and bondholder groups will consent to a forbearance agreement but want something in return, like more collateral, personal guarantees, or cash in order to make it happen.

I'm involved in many bond restructures because the holders of the bonds forced me on the debtor the moment he violated the debt coverage ratio of his bond. This ratio is meant to justify the bondholders' decision to insert someone like me into the company. No matter what the covenant in your bank document, always build in cure periods to allow you time to repair your ratios and get back in compliance before the creditor can interfere. This is the single most powerful ratio that a bank inserts in a document so that they can bring in a financial advisor, raise your interest rate, or force you to restructure. Many of my former clients—from the smallest nonprofit to charter schools to receiverships to huge corporations and manufacturers—were losing money, and since they failed the test of this ratio their bankers were able to force my involvement in their businesses.

Bank documents are an important element of your bank relationships, but you need to make sure that you're both being fair to the person giving you money and acting in the best interests of your business. That means rereading bank documents annually, avoiding evergreen clauses, and insisting upon cure periods in your financial covenants. Again, though your banker may not be thrilled at not getting his way, he will respect that you are aware of your banking and fiduciary obligations and acting wisely on behalf of your company. In this way, you will grow and foster a healthy and successful bank relationship that follows and respects The 10 C's of Bank Relationships for CEOs.

Chapter 5

Fraud: Stop It Before It Starts

Have you ever found any fraud at your company?

If not, then you're probably not looking hard enough.

The goal of this chapter is to inspire you to create more checks and balances on the financial processes at your business. I want you to keep your eyes open, thereby deterring fraud or allowing you to catch it far earlier and more often than you otherwise might. This chapter is packed with tips for preventing fraud. Pick any three of them to implement this year, and you'll be safer. Add another five the following year, and I'll be pleased. If you can get to all of them and show me, I'll enter you into my Proactive Business Owner of the Year sweepstakes.

Create an Official Fraud Policy

First thing's first: you need a Fraud Policy, and this chapter should convince you of its paramount necessity. I'm disheartened, though never surprised, when I ask clients and groups of CEOs if they have official fraud policies, because the answer is inevitably and overwhelmingly no. The reason I'm disheartened is because there's hardly a task so easy in this entire book as creating and implementing a fraud policy. The main reason I find that companies don't implement fraud policies is because CEOs are embarrassed and reluctant to prosecute employees who steal.

A fraud policy is similar to a mission statement and core values. Most companies have at least a mission statement, which explains why the company exists and what its higher purpose is. Core values further flesh out a company's attitude and unique approach that are indispensable to its operations; they might deal with product quality, customer service, charity and so forth. Some retail chains, like Whole Foods, even display their mission statement and core values on huge signs near the checkout area. Many companies spend tens of thousands of dollars hiring consultants to perfectly craft their mission and values, yet they don't take even an extra $50 to create a clear and official fraud policy for all to see—the policy that outlines the approach a company takes towards those who commit fraud, steal, lie, or cheat.

Fraud policies are very easy to craft and quite direct. "If you steal, you will be prosecuted to the fullest extent of the law." In addition to being posted publicly, this should be written in the employee manual or handbook, and every employee—including all relatives working for the company—should have to sign it and acknowledge its receipt. Catching (and prosecuting!) an employee committing fraud or stealing will deter a surprisingly high percentage of your remaining workforce from even considering theft.

If Someone Commits Fraud, Prosecute Them

Some people flinch when they hear me say that they have to prosecute those who steal from them, and I think that's out of remorse. I've read fraud-related articles that claim that 75 percent of people who are caught stealing and committing fraud and subsequently prosecuted for it are first-time offenders. It's rare that they were actually first-time offenders! In most cases they were simply never prosecuted by those who caught and fired them when it happened previously. I've seen too many CEOs flinch with remorse at the thought of not having prosecuted perpetrators in the past. Though we may assume that CEOs prosecute those who steal from them, that's not the case. Prosecuting is easier said than done, especially when we know the violator and perhaps regard him as a friend.

People don't prosecute for a few reasons. First, it's hard to prosecute people we know well. At huge companies the CEO doesn't know hourly workers on the floor, but he knows the CFO, sales manager, or other high-level financial staff who have worked for him for years. It may be easy to fire and even prosecute someone who carries a little product out the back door, but we are more inclined to be forgiving when those we work with daily steal. We worry about messing up their lives and the lives of their families, who we may also know. Second, prosecuting seems like a messy business. It creates paperwork, involves lawyers, and consumes time, energy, and money. My clients say, "I've lost enough already, and it's unlikely I'll recover enough to make it worth the effort." Third, people don't prosecute because they think having someone successfully steal from them is embarrassing. They don't want others to know, whether employees, the public, friends, or family. As understandable as each of these justifications for not prosecuting may seem, none of them is a good reason for not actually prosecuting thieves and perpetrators of fraud.

Here are the reasons why you should prosecute anyone who steals.

1. **In the long run, it benefits everyone.** Not prosecuting doesn't just allay the concerns outlined above—it has far-reaching consequences for the larger business world. When CEOs prosecute fraudsters it benefits everyone, from employers and the industry to the average honest worker who deserves a job for which he's not competing against thieves.

2. **You could find yourself in trouble legally if you don't.** What will you do if you're called for a reference for a new job for one of your thieving workers? This is delicate territory, legally.

Put yourself in a position to tell the truth, and let other employers make informed decisions about who to hire.

3. **It reflects poorly on you and your company if you don't prosecute:** You undermine your fraud policy and send a message to others that it has no teeth. You invite people to steal from you and lose their jobs … not a big deal when compared to prison.

4. **A strong, enforced fraud policy strengthens your bank relationships.** No banker is comforted by the fact that money could be stolen from one of his clients, but he will rest assured in the knowledge that anyone stealing from you will be prosecuted in an attempt to recover what was stolen, as well as damages. Would you rather protect the interests of someone who lied and took your money, or those of the person whose relationship is built on honesty and who supplies you with money in your time of need?

5. **If you don't, they will steal again.** I've got dozens of examples of controllers, CFOs, warehouse managers, and payroll clerks who were never prosecuted when they were originally caught stealing, and nearly every one of them stole again, eventually. I know, because I'm the one who caught them and then finally had them prosecuted. In one case a bookkeeper at a church

in New York stole millions of dollars from the church. She had done the same thing at a previous church in another state, but because that church chose not to prosecute, she just relocated and started stealing again.

So I'll reiterate: those who are discovered committing fraud for the first time probably aren't first-time offenders. They're just getting caught for the first time and, because you chose to do the right thing, prosecuted.

Leverage the Value of an Informal Fraud Policy

Even if you don't have an official fraud policy (though perhaps you paused earlier, wrote up your Fraud Policy and sent it off to the printer to make you a 14' x 4' banner for your warehouse, office, or store) and you haven't opted to prosecute offenders in the past, you may find that you have an informal —or psychological—fraud policy. Though I insist that an official, written, and ostentatiously displayed fraud policy is important, I'm happy knowing that you at least have an informal fraud policy. An informal fraud policy is one that is implied by your actions and your business environment—like security systems and cameras—but that is not directly stated.

I once ran a retail chain based in Delaware at which the shrinkage was 5-6 percent. For a company doing $100 million annually, that was $6 million a year missing. Obviously I couldn't catch every person who was individually stealing from the warehouse or off the floor, but I had other options. I only needed to catch a few perps to make my point. Before I arrived, when a cashier or sales associate was caught stealing, the manager would have that person quietly escorted out the back, loaded into a police car, and inconspicuously taken to jail. He didn't want to alarm customers, make a big deal of the problem or face the public embarrassment of poor hiring decisions. Once I started running this operation and I caught someone stealing, the process went differently. I would have multiple police officers parade the perpetrator on a circuitous route through the store in handcuffs. The police cars would be out front, lights swirling and sirens blaring, and the thief would usually be crying and embarrassed. I wanted everyone to see, from employees to customers to management, that you could choose to steal from our store, but if I caught you, I would do everything in my power to make you regret it. That informal fraud policy resulted in a shrinkage reduction of 50 percent in the first month. Over the course of the year that translated into $3 million saved because people were scared and knew they'd be embarrassed and prosecuted for stealing. You don't have to catch everyone who's stealing—you have to make everyone believe that it's not worth getting caught.

At another assignment, I had a ton of merchandise walking out the back door of a warehouse. Once again, I couldn't catch everyone red-handed, and I didn't have time or the money to install a sophisticated system on an interim basis, so I had to try something else. I "installed" a camera next to each of the ten doors; I just drilled a hole in the wall and fed a wire through it with a battery-operated red light right next to it. The camera and wire didn't go anywhere—and neither did my merchandise after that. The camera functioned as a psychological theft deterrent that scared those who considered stealing. After reducing shrinkage, I had the money to upgrade the security and improve the inventory tag system.

As I've mentioned before, the sports bar chain had plenty of problems, and two of those problems were related to fraud, both at the bottom rungs of the employment ladder and at the top. We noticed that food and alcohol costs were way too high at a disproportionate number of locations. Upon investigation, it turned out that employees were taking food and liquor out to the dumpsters behind their restaurants during their shifts and then returning later at night to pick up their stashes. After we alerted managers of the way inventory was walking out of our restaurants, we reduced theft through public terminations and subsequent prosecutions.

No matter your business, employees and professionals will find creative ways of draining the company's resources for personal gain. It's never fun, but you have to assume the worst and watch the back door. Being a proactive leader means considering all of the vulnerabilities in your organization and plugging them up with the kinds of informal fraud policies that deter theft and fraud. Whether or not you have an official fraud policy in place right now, I encourage you to think about your informal fraud policies and whether or not they have the right psychological effects. Make sure to leverage your informal fraud policy to prevent theft and prosecute those who do steal.

Keep Your Security Room Locked

An unfortunate problem associated with informal fraud policies is the tendency people have to undermine them in foolish ways. I was working on a company in Dallas where all the surveillance equipment was kept in one room. Fortunately for those interested in doing wrong by the company, this so-called surveillance room was kept unlocked at all times. This incident predates our current era of digital data automatically uploaded to secure servers and retained for months. It was back in the days of videocassettes that kept data in one place at one time until someone erased it. After someone stole something at this company, he could walk right into the surveillance room and change or erase the tape. In one notable case, a thief just paused the tape while he did his business and then politely restarted it when he was through.

I encourage you to have security equipment, but make sure to keep the door to your security room locked. If a truly excellent thief is determined to hack in, then perhaps you're dealing with issues beyond the scope of this book, but a simple deadbolt that keeps people from just strolling in at their leisure does more than you think. Secure your security equipment.

Give Your CFO or Corporate Controller a Break

Require your CFO to take two consecutive weeks of vacation each year. During his absence, do his job. Sit at his desk. Open his mail. Review all of the deposits. Talk to his secretary or assistant. Just see what happens. This method has long been highly successful for CEOs, and banks have used this same technique for ages. If you don't find anything unusual, that's wonderful. Unfortunately, though, you might uncover a detail worth noticing.

Once, while sitting at a CFO's desk, I decided to open his mail. Lo and behold—he was having his Cayman Islands bank account statements sent to his office. Are you kidding me? The man was embezzling money from the company and had the detailed statements of those embezzlements sent to his office address. Considering all he was stealing I think he could have afforded a PO Box. Another sit-down at a CFO's desk who I suspected of fraud got me poking around his computer. I discovered a spreadsheet with all of the money he'd stolen in one of the few folders on his desktop. Everything was dated and tracked. Sometimes it's like thieves just giftwrap their crime for you. If people feel so comfortable at your company that they are getting stolen money bank statements at the office and leaving the details of their thievery on their desktops in non-password protected files then you need to seriously reconsider your fraud policy.

CFOs and controllers are in the most opportune positions to steal, able to set audit parameters that enable wrongdoing, and least suspected due to their high corporate titles. As the person governing all of the finances at your business, you must learn from the disastrous mistakes of past CEOs and keep your eyes on your CFO. At the very least, this kind of supervision will allow you to stay better attuned to your company's financial situation.

The majority of CFOs or controllers can also be extremely useful in finding fraud throughout your company. Use their expertise and that of your CPA for creative solutions. I maintain contact with several CFOs who "get it" and were instrumental in our turning around a business.

Always Have Someone Double-Check the Payroll

CFOs aren't the only people at your company who might be stealing. How often do you double-check the payroll? I often recommend that people engage the services of a payroll processing company because it's generally the least likely avenue to take that will result in fraud as long as a second party verifies the payroll. All you do is enter employee hours or salaries into the system and everybody gets paid on Friday. People have their reasons for not using a payroll service, but whatever the reason, if you do payroll in-house, make sure someone is double-checking the work. Otherwise, you may have an Aunt Tess on your hands.

Aunt Tess was a payroll clerk I once had the pleasure of encountering. She'd been working at the same company doing the payroll for more than twenty-five years, and everybody loved Aunt Tess. I suspected something was fishy when Aunt Tess came into work the day after an appendectomy to do the payroll. There she was, just handing out paychecks as if eighteen hours earlier she hadn't been split open, unconscious on an operating table. I inquired and learned that Aunt Tess had a nearly miraculous and uncanny ability to be at work for every payroll. Indeed, in twenty-five years Aunt Tess had not missed one single payroll day. Not one. Apparently she even took her vacations around payroll. What a loyal employee! Devoted as that may seem, that kind of behavior is suspicious in my book, and it threw up a red flag.

At a big company, no one knows all the hourly people's names, and this was a fact that Aunt Tess had been methodically exploiting for a quarter of a century. As it turned out, she'd created a handful of specious hourly employees, whose concocted existence allowed her to steal between $75,000 and $100,000 annually. Considering the love for Aunt Tess, everyone was quite shocked to learn of this betrayal, but no matter how beloved your payroll clerk (or any member of your financial staff), always have someone else double-check the payroll. Oh, and astonishingly, Aunt Tess was never prosecuted for her misdeeds. She only made restitution of $100,000 that remained from the millions she stole during her employment!

Don't Rehire People Who Steal From You

If you couldn't believe that people didn't prosecute those who stole from them, you'll gasp at the fact that I have to say this: never—ever—rehire people who steal from you. If I've seen this happen at companies that I turnaround, I can't imagine how much it's happening out there in the wider business world.

I was once retained to assess a company and discovered that the sales manager had a scheme with a customer. The published price of this company's primary widget was $8.50. The sales manager would place an order for the customer, ship the merchandise, and then go to accounts receivable and process a credit memo for that customer which would net him a price of $7.50 per widget. The customer would then slip the manager 50 percent of his $1 savings ($1/widget). When it's only one of hundreds of customers, schemes like this can go undetected for a long time. I got lucky, however, and discovered this was happening because the manager got greedy and began his thievery with multiple customers. In his hastiness to reap the benefits of the company's ignorance, he put a credit through for the wrong company, whose honest accounting department promptly disclosed the error. Upon researching the credit we discovered this fraud, and the whole scheme unraveled. Aside from the mandatory prosecution, you would think that this was the end of the story.

It's true that the sales manager was fired, but he was never prosecuted after I left, despite my putting the wheels in motion. In his absence, sales declined by 25 percent because apparently, our thieving sales manager was also generating a great deal of full-priced business. Bully for him. Unable to find a suitable sales force to replace this one guy, one year later the CEO rehired the once-thieving salesman. When asked why he rehired him, the CEO explained to me that the salesman had found God, repented his sins, and begged forgiveness. Though he never made monetary restitution for his misguided ways, he nonetheless apologized sufficiently enough for the CEO, who gave him a second chance in order to return the company's sales to a profitable level. Six months later the salesman finally went to jail for stealing—again.

I believe in second chances in life. We all screw up at one point or another, and I dare say, we all deserve to find forgiveness. Despite that, do not rehire people who steal from you. If you think that you might not be able to enforce this rule because you're such a forgiving person, then put it in your company's bylaws to prohibit you from rehiring thieves. People who knowingly rehire those who steal from them deserve everything they have coming.

Tighten Up Your Checks and Balances

Payroll isn't the only expense on which you need to keep tighter controls. I want you to start rethinking all of your financial processes and replacing them with more thorough checks and balances. Any place money or goods exist or move is a place that fraud or theft could occur. Once you accept that and appreciate that no one is above suspicion, the better off your company will be. As Aunt Tess claimed, it wasn't personal. She didn't think she was stealing from a person—the company's owner—or betraying her fellow employees. She just thought she was stealing from a company. Her attitude towards the anonymity of her "victim" will make even the most seemingly loyal of employees be the reason your shrink rate is high or the cause of inexplicable invoices—which brings me to expense reports.

Generally, expense reports undergo a fairly straightforward process of getting handed into the appropriate department, reviewed by the person in charge, checked off, and paid out. However, what I've seen is that for every salesman and consultant who has his expense reports checked, a C-level or senior employee's expense reports are glossed over. Sometimes the CFO is even writing his own expense reimbursement check, and that's a problem that must be addressed. All systems require checks and balances, and when it's assumed that senior managers' and officers' expenses don't require review you're going to run into problems. After all, you did just read the word "assume," and that's when your eyebrows should rise.

The CFO at a manufacturing company in Wilmington, DE knew that the golden audit number for an automatically reviewed expense was $5,000. So he was writing himself tens of thousands of dollars in expense-related checks, each in the mid $4,000 range. I suspected unsavory behavior was happening because the CFO dragged his feet about getting us the information we wanted during our review process. Uncooperative personnel, especially at that level, always catch my attention. Part of my review process at any company losing money is perusing the expense reports of senior people, and the CFO's behavior placed this exercise on the front burner. What I found was $180,000 worth of recent fraud, and whatever else was buried in the past.

One element of the company's mistake that allowed the CFO to perpetrate this fraud for so long was that all expense-related checks took two signatures. On the surface, this is an excellent policy. However, when I reviewed this process, I noticed that the co-signor wasn't double-checking what he was signing. Check signing cannot be a perfunctory job; the signer must understand the gravity of what he or she is doing. That person must also feel comfortable asking questions and bringing concerns straight to the CEO. As the leader of your company, you should have a personal relationship with whoever signs checks. Make that individual feel personally responsible to you and like you are always available for anything he or she needs.

In addition to conveying the importance of this job, I want to emphasize the need to change the standard by which you review transactions. Auditors often set the level at which transactions are reviewed (in this case, $5,000). Though auditors will occasionally spot check just below that number, make sure they're regularly sampling at least 80 percent below the transaction standard. I've found that to be, more or less, the sweet spot of those committing this kind of fraud.

No company is immune to fraud. Just recently the Woodruff Arts Center, the largest cultural organization in Atlanta, was embezzled to the tune of $1.48 million. Seems that a mid-level administrator made up a fake company, and submitted invoices from that company for five years. The CEO was quoted as saying, "The amounts billed and paid to the company increased over time but remained under limits that might have drawn attention."

No matter what limits you've set for your company, when you're shelling out hundreds of thousands of dollars a year to any one vendor, make sure someone is paying attention.

Check and Recheck Those Checks and Balances

I want to emphasize the importance of not just putting checks and balances in place, but also conveying the absolute necessity of regularly rechecking and rebalancing those checks and balances. It is this kind of vigilance that ultimately deters and catches fraud. Regularity fosters complacence, and complacence is a breeding ground for fraud. I encourage you to be an unpredictable maverick with your financial checks and balances.

As we're taught in school, the US government has checks and balances via our well crafted Constitution and the division of governmental responsibilities into our legislative, executive, and judicial branches. At times it may seem inefficient, but I assure you that it's a brilliantly conceived system. Those checks and balances are designed to prevent the abuse of power, which is exactly the same as preventing fraud. Fraud is an abuse of the power placed in the hands of those you and your company—or the electorate—opts to trust. In most cases, that pertains in some fashion or another to stealing money, but all fraud can be boiled down to an abuse of power.

I insist on checks and balances in all areas of money and finance because checks and balances generally prevent fraud by covering weak spots in a system. Crooks are creative, or at least they have a knack for seeing the flaw in a system and subsequently exploiting it. The more checks and balances, the fewer weaknesses and the less potential for fraud.

One objection I often hear about additional checks and balances is that they require more personnel or better-credentialed employees who are able to juggle these additional responsibilities. That is, checks and balances are an expense. Is fraud not also an expense? I'd rather spend money and time preventing fraud than spend at least the same amount figuring out where my company's money is going. Consider preventative care in medicine. Rather than seek care when you're already sick, focus on a healthy lifestyle to minimize illness in the first place. Going to the hospital sick can be incredibly expensive, but the regular cost of preventative care reduces expensive doctors visits and catches illnesses and infections sooner to minimize their costly impacts. Take the preventative care attitude towards fraud and set in place as many checks and balances as you can. It always pays to prevent fraud.

Take All Shortages Seriously

One of the most common checks and balances in retail locations with checkout counters and cash drawers is counting the drawers every night. Counting lets cash be compared to receipts. However, drawers are often inexact, and it can be easy for managers and owners to get complacent and accept a standard over or under. I understand that if you're balancing out $100,000 in revenue and find that you're $86 off, you might just want to let it go, as the trouble of figuring out what happened to the $86 is not worth the $86.

But what if someone had stolen that $86? What if that person stole $86 every day? Arguably, that changes the value of the initial $86, since this missing money is unlikely to be a one-time occurrence, but rather a recurring and augmenting "expense."

Now imagine that you have a single drawer that's off by $14 one day. That happens, especially at a place that does enough business in cash on each drawer. However, if that happens on the same drawer at a big department store five days in a row, the cashier on that drawer is going to get fired for one of two reasons. Either he's incompetent or he's stealing. But there's a third potential reason: someone else in-house is stealing from him because he's unsuspecting.

Many employees know that a drawer can be off by $20 a day without raising suspicion, so they use other cashiers' drawers to give their friends $10 too much change. By rotating whose drawers they're using, it becomes difficult to catch these slightly more sophisticated thieves. I encourage you to watch for patterns and consistencies, like cross referencing who's regularly working on days that show higher than usual collective shortages, even if those shortages don't appear on their drawers.

Many companies grow lax on the acceptability of shortages, but don't make the mistake of ignoring the systems you have in place. You put them there for a reason. Take all shortages seriously.

Always Poke Around Your Books

Investigating shortages is just one piece of the larger financial job of all CEOs: regularly investigating the books. When a company starts out, the CEO or business owner signs all of the checks. As a company grows and other people—like the CFO, controller, auditor—start signing checks, the CEO or a majority shareholder should still double-check what's getting paid and to whom. The occasional perusal of a ledger, checkbook, or QuickBooks will show you where money is going. Ask questions about that money. How often are we paying for X? With what does company Y supply us?

Even if you don't find fraud, you'll likely discover unnecessary expenses, which is more common in these cases. Employees in accounts payable aren't always informed when a piece of leased equipment is sold or returned or when suppliers are changed. Numerous payables and other bills are put on autopilot and not even reviewed annually. I go through a company's expenses line by line, questioning everything with the CEO and check-signer, often finding thousands—if not tens or even hundreds of thousands—of dollars worth of expenses being paid that don't need to be. In one company I discovered that they were still paying for a leased copier that they hadn't had in over twelve years!

> **Ask questions about that money. How often are we paying for X? With what does company Y supply us?**

When perusing your books like a proactive CEO, you may uncover fraud lurking around them. While doing a sort in an Excel spreadsheet on vendor addresses trying to cut freight costs and save money, we stumbled upon two vendors, one in California and one in Indiana, doing business with our main store in Chattanooga. It would have made sense that there were vendors in California and Indiana to attend to our subsidiaries, but it didn't make sense that we were sending checks to these companies at a PO Box in Chattanooga—which, I reiterate, is where our headquarters was.

It turns out that the controller had created dummy vendors, and he was cutting checks to them for amounts between $50 and $100. He would then collect these checks at his local Chattanooga PO Box and deposit them in the name of these dummy vendors in accounts in Chattanooga that only he controlled. Over the course of ten years this controller stole over a million dollars. An auditor would never find such small transactions, and we only discovered them because the CEO and I were poking around in the books trying to come up with useful ways of extracting unique, money-saving information. It worked, too, since we saved $250,000 a year.

While turning around Chapter 22 Books, I discovered deposits being made into a Discover Card merchant account (the account that accepts customers' Discover cards). This account should have been canceled when the company changed merchant banks, but it was not and was instead included in another set of books, which was being used to fund one employee's mortgage. How does something like this go unnoticed for years? I only stumbled upon it one month that sales were down, and I started investigating. For whatever reason, Discover Card charges accounted for nearly 30 percent of sales that month rather than the usual couple of percentage points. This huge dip stood out, and I realized that we still took Discover but that it wasn't showing up on our books. Routinely check all of your transactions and payments, and whether fraud or unnecessary expenses, you're bound to find something worth looking at twice.

Regularly Monitor and Review Monetary Trends

There's more to poking around your books than simply finding expenses that no longer need paying. You should also be reviewing monetary trends religiously. Figure out what kinds of numbers matter to you and your business—shrinkage, scrap, manufacturing cost per widget, a particular line (or lines) on your P&L—and determine what range those numbers should fall in to indicate to you that your operation is running smoothly. Next, generate Key Indicator or Flash Reports, via your accounting software that will regularly provide you with this data. Finally, graph the data over time to look for trends and to know when the data is out of the zone of acceptability for your business.

At a couture dress manufacturer in New York, the CEO should have been watching the company's scrap and cost per dress of manufacturing. In the world of couture, the profit per unit is generally quite high. That margin is ruined, however, when the production manager takes the overrun of $5,000 dresses and sells them to discount operations, especially when he starts buying more materials to make more "overrun" dresses and writes off the whole process to scrap materials.

Had the CEO been regularly monitoring his scrap rate or actual rather than budgeted cost per dress in the manufacturing process—and then questioning what seemed out of the ordinary—he would have noticed an out-of-whack expense line much earlier. If you are making a widget and you know the material costs X and the labor costs Y, you need to watch the trends to make sure that your numbers are staying consistent (or inconsistent in your favor). You can only do this if you have a method in place for regularly monitoring and reviewing monetary trends.

A few years ago I got a call at 2 a.m. and was told by my plant manager in North Carolina that there was a dangerous oil spill at our plant. Eager to avoid a major catastrophe with the Environmental Protection Agency, I jumped into my car and drove to North Carolina in the middle of the night. I made it there in record time, hoping to contain the spill by sun-up. As we entered the plant, two hundred Uzi rounds were fired in our general direction but fortunately, ricocheted off the hundreds of steel tanks in the plant.

Later that day after we'd spoken with a policeman, he came over, pulled his shades down to his nose and looked me in the eyes. "If my union buddies on the railroad had meant to kill you, you'd be dead. I recommend you get back in your fancy car, and get your ass back to Atlanta." So, why did I get shot at? For the same reason that the couture manufacturer found himself in trouble: because the CEO of this oil company wasn't reviewing his own trends. (Like I said, I get shot at because I clean up the messes of CEOs who are not proactive.) In this case, the CEO wasn't watching his demurrage charges from the railroad. Demurrage charges are the fines levied by the railroad for not offloading your cargo and cars quickly enough. The company was getting its oil off-loaded from its railroad cars, but the railroad workers who were supposed to move the cars afterwards weren't moving them, and the charges kept adding up. Believe it or not, the oil company actually did have financial controls in place to be notified if certain expenses were occurring at an unreasonable rate, which is great, but worthless if you ignore the notifications on those controls for eighteen months.

When I arrived at this oil company, I started asking questions about hundreds of thousands of dollars in demurrage costs, which seemed outrageous to me. The railroad investigated and found that the three employees who were supposed to be moving these cars after we emptied them were actually fishing, goofing off, and generally not doing their jobs. One employee was fired, and two were suspended as a result of my investigation. They retaliated against the oil company by breaking an external oil valve and releasing thousands of gallons of oil, which were heading towards a nearby stream—hello, EPA!—and that brought me there during pajama hours. And then the shooting began. The long-term cause of my getting shot at was the oil company ignoring its demurrage charges, but the short-term cause was that people who weren't doing their jobs wanted to continue not doing their jobs.

The lesson here goes back to being proactive and having proper financial controls, but what good are financial controls if you ignore them? Put your policies in place and follow them. Regularly monitor and review monetary trends, and don't ignore the results.

Do Not Skew the Facts

We already know there is no better policy with your banker than honesty. Unfortunately, the CEO of a hard drive manufacturer in California did not feel the same way. He desperately wanted a line of credit from his bank for $60 million, so he stuffed the channel in order to make his company appear worthy. Stuffing the channel is when a manufacturer oversells product to put sales on the books, despite knowing that much of the merchandise will be returned unsold; this inflates the books by overstating the top line, thereby improving the bottom line—at least temporarily. This strategy, if it can be called that, is a "timing" play for short-term gain.

This strategy led to the loan this CEO wanted, but when the company repurchased the inventory in the channel within sixty days, it became out of compliance on the line of credit. Once the bank defaulted on the company I was brought in to salvage what I could and to hopefully restructure the company. It survived thanks to a hedge fund loan, but the CEO lost his job because he skewed the facts.

Q-Zar provides another instance of a CEO skewing the facts to get the deal he wanted. When laser-tag equipment still had a very high value, the company that was trying to acquire Q-Zar sought a large loan to make its deal work. The inventory on Q-Zar's books was overstated, a "reality" achieved by adding the inventory in its Ireland-based location to the corporate financial statements. The Canadian auditors never verified the inventory and thus, the bank granted the company a far larger loan than it could handle.

When the company filed for Chapter 11, I was brought in as CEO; within weeks in my new position I visited the Ireland "plant" only to discover it was a vacant lot. The more than $50 million inventory was a figment of the president and CFO's imagination. I immediately went to the judge to convert the case to a Chapter 7 rather than try to bring the company through the bankruptcy and be embarrassed by the fraud. The creditors sued the accounting firm and collected millions of dollars from faulty accounting, once again highlighting the blunder of skewing facts. (The president had left the country and the CFO had a heart attack and died before his trial.) Learn from these CEOs' mistakes and resist manipulating data. Consider the fact that the kinds of rules that prevent companies from getting loans that they can't handle are in place for a reason. Both cases illustrate a flaw in the CEOs' characters.

Match Purchase Orders Against Invoices

I want to stress another area of the accounts payable department that has a tendency to get put on autopilot for ease of management. It may seem like I'm picking on accounts payable, but problems that arise there are not necessarily because that department isn't paying attention. In this case, it's because accounts payable is but one cog in the larger ordering wheel. Rarely is the same person counting incoming shipments and matching POs to packing slips as is paying the invoices. Though there are sometimes processes in place to prevent this from being haphazard, there is almost always room for error and exploitation.

At a company in Jacksonville, FL the selling agent and the controller were working together on a little scheme. The purchasing agent at an oil company was buying one hundred railroad cars of oil a month, each holding 20,000 gallons. After a car was purchased, the selling agent would divert the car and its oil to a competitor. The original company would be invoiced and paid for the oil it never received and the competitor was also invoiced but would pay a discounted rate. The controller and purchasing agent were splitting that discount. The people getting ripped off the most were the companies being unjustly invoiced, but they would have caught the problem much sooner had they been matching POs and delivery tickets.

Once an invoice is in your system it's on autopilot, so be sure to check all incoming shipments and invoices against POs to ensure you're paying only for what you get. You'll catch honest mistakes made by your vendors, but if you find a scheme like this, you'll be grateful for this check and balance in your fraud policy.

Consider the Financial Impact of Rare Events on Your Business

By comparison to the ease of checking POs against invoices, it's incredibly challenging to detect what I call off-book transactions. An off-book transaction happens as the result of a rare occurrence. Say, for instance there's an extraordinary event like a fire or a theft, and you claim $25,000 in damages and loss from your insurance company. The check they send, though, is not part of the normal course of events at your business—a fact known by the person who receives the check. So, that person, who we'll say for the sake of argument (and my experience) is the CFO, takes the check and deposits it, not into the company's normal account, but into an account at a different bank under your company's name that he set up. There's now $25,000 in a bank account, but only the CFO knows about it. Auditors don't know this is happening because it's an extraordinary non-recurring event that stays off-book. Nobody knows to look for what isn't missing.

This doesn't just happen with insurance checks. Off-book fraud happens with rebates, spiffs (sale performance incentive plans), or other money that is rare enough that accountants and auditors don't know to monitor it. A pre-purchased rebate is another opportunity for an off-book transaction. One large printing company I turned around used to buy millions of dollars in paper every year, and a new vendor offered an annual contract at a million dollars in purchases with a $100,000 signing bonus.

When the rebate check arrived, the CFO deposited it in the business's name, but in an off-book bank account. Since the auditors aren't involved with these kinds of contracts, they had no idea that they should have been looking for the rebate check. I caught this because I felt compelled to review a contract that represented such a large percentage of expenditures, but for every huge rebate that is uncovered there are ten others under $10,000 that get missed.

The challenge with off-book transactions is their infrequency: at best they arise annually. If I'm around a company long enough to witness the recurrence of an annual cycle I'm more likely to catch off-book transactions, but if I'm not, then it's up to others to alert auditors (and more than one of them, mind you) to be on the lookout for rare or annual occurrences that could be slipping the books. For instance, I had a controller who would intentionally overpay insurance premiums. The auditors would see regular checks to the insurance company, but never consider that they were over-paid and therefore soon to be followed by refund checks. The controller was depositing the refunds elsewhere.

People will take advantage of what they know will be out of sight and out of mind, so I encourage you to watch the unusual with your own eyes and follow it from start to finish.

Trust Your Instincts

Watching the unusual is part of trusting your instincts, which is my final fraud prevention tip. If something seems fishy, trust your instincts and investigate further. It's your business—or at least it's in your charge—and you don't have to feel guilty about questioning processes, transactions, or people.

I recall a manufacturing company in Columbia, SC, that was making dresses for an outlet mall chain. Shrinkage shot up, but I couldn't figure out why. I thought it was just uncoordinated and miscellaneous theft, but as I couldn't manage to stop it, I had to trust my instincts and take a drastic step. I hired a private detective to spy on the warehouse, and he uncovered the magnitude of the operation going on behind my back. The warehouse manager of the company had a nasty gambling habit and owed the loan shark several hundred thousand dollars from gambling debts. To pay his debt, he was loading his truck with merchandise at night and on weekends, and selling the merchandise for cash that he then paid the loan shark to reduce his debt. As in all fraud cases, I'm glad I trusted my instincts. If anyone ever tells you what you must absolutely do or not do, accept or ignore, that's also a good sign to look closer. Absolutes from employees nudge my instincts towards further investigation.

Another case in which my instincts alerted me to a very unique fraud was at the sports bar chain. I mentioned already that there were two kinds of fraud at the company: one low level and one corporate level. We've already talked about watching your back door, but what about your priceless memorabilia? As a sports bar and restaurant, it is one of those places that covers the walls in memorabilia, like autographed photos of athletes, their used sports equipment, jerseys and the like. One afternoon I found myself sitting in the corporate offices admiring the autographed photos and jerseys that adorned the walls; I was wondering what the best way to sell off these valuables would be because I had to generate cash quickly. As I stared, I noticed that the "t" in a lot of the signatures looked weirdly similar. I'm no graphologist, but I couldn't shake this weird feeling. I made a phone call and hired a certified graphologist to analyze the signatures and another expert to assess the value of the memorabilia. As I started asking questions in the meantime, I learned that all of the memorabilia had been purchased through a connection of one of the board members for hundreds of thousands of dollars. Wouldn't you know, it all turned out to be fake.

I was hired to do an assessment at an auto parts business east of the Mississippi that wasn't doing too well. The CEO, let's call her Olivia, was very bright and had been recruited from California. Her husband had stayed there and she flew back and forth every few weeks.

My gut was telling me something wasn't right but I wasn't sure what it was. I found a catalog for a women's clothing company based on the West Coast on her desk but didn't think much about it. Then while I was researching that same company, her name came up again.

On a hunch I called the company and asked to speak to Olivia. "She's traveling but you can speak to her secretary," I was told. When her secretary answered the phone, I asked what Olivia's position with the company was. "She's the CEO," the secretary replied.

Olivia had decided the auto parts business wasn't for her, so she took another job as CEO. Except she forgot to quit her old job. We took care of that for her.

Fraud is a shame, but it is nonetheless a part of the business world. Trust your instincts, put checks and balances in place wherever you can, and regularly review and monitor your numbers and processes. With this approach, you are less likely to be the victim of fraud, or you will at least catch it before it becomes ruinous.

Chapter 6

The Big Picture

The central role of any CEO is to maintain an understanding of the big picture. He must know about the details, too, and ask copious questions of his team, while always sustaining a keen grasp on the larger plan and picture. Life and business often get in the way, obscuring the big picture from view. Other distractions—like "the next big thing"—divert the CEO's attention from the task at hand. Opportunities like a huge client or contract are appealing for their ability to send business through the roof, but be cautious in your pursuit. The wonder product that sells faster than it can be kept on the shelves is a tempting allure, but let this chapter serve as a warning about that which seems so great and shiny. Whatever you do and no matter how big the opportunity, I want to make sure that you never fall in love with a deal or a product. Love blinds people—it makes them bet the ranch and lean too heavily on the Big Gorilla. These are classic CEO mistakes, and even the best can fall prey to their allure.

It's true that big risks and gambles sometimes pay off—of course they do. However, as the leader of your company you have a responsibility to keep your eye on the ball and to maintain an objective bird's eye view. Can you do both of those things at the same time? If not, you might not be the leader you think, and it might be time to learn some lessons from past CEOs who thought that everything great rested in one singular matter or affair. Each of the CEOs in my stories became too dependent, and each of them subsequently paid the price with the loss of his job, his business, and his dreams. Let's learn from their mistakes.

Stay Ahead of Change by Embracing Change

I often find myself musing that if more CEOs had degrees in history than MBAs then I would have less work to do. One thing that most historians understand—especially those who can keep the big picture in sight while focusing on the details—is that history is cyclical. (Physicists also fare well in this department because they know that everything that goes up must come down; nothing rises forever.) Historians see the ups and downs that take place throughout the historical timeline. They see civilizations of once-great promise and power rising and falling. America has been on the ascendency for quite a while, yet from the inside it can be challenging to see its trajectory along the lines of history.

> Stay ahead of change by embracing change. Many companies ride the wave of what's working and worry about problems once the wave crashes on the shore.

The same is true for a CEO and his business, and that's what makes this kind of visualization and perspective essential for the great CEO. CEOs who understand this rise and fall, this ebb and flow, this give and take of power, this seesaw of good and bad times, can better understand the challenges of sustained success.

One of the most significant factors of this perspective is knowing that good times don't last because change is always on the horizon. This is not pessimistic but a realist's preparations for a variety of outcomes and eventualities. Seize the opportunities of the good times, but don't lean on the joy they bring as an excuse to avoid preparing yourself and your company via checks and balances and controls and processes that will protect you when business doesn't go as hoped. Stay ahead of change by embracing change. Many companies ride the wave of what's working and worry about problems once the wave crashes on the shore. That's the wrong approach, and you should learn from CEOs who lead their companies this way. As long as you know it's a wave, you know it will end. Like a talented surfer, come smoothly onto the shore, having already scanned the horizon for the next wave. If you don't see another wave, have a contingency plan and evolve.

The great CEO doesn't always have the most profitable company, but he is protecting the financial integrity of his company and taking proactive steps during a downturn so that he can prepare to better profit when there is an upturn. The moment you foresee a downturn, take the opportunity to see what is inefficient in your business by eliminating loss leaders and reducing inventory; review niche pricing on market leader widgets and increase marketing and sales expenses in high profit-margin areas. By shoring up problems during a downturn, you prepare your company to run lean and mean at all times. These are the moves of CEOs who see the big picture. They are not caught up in either the good times or the bad times. They understand the temporary nature of history, empires, nations, and, of course, companies. This is the kind of perspective you need to cultivate and keep in mind as I warn you about the many factors that compromise your vantage point.

Beware of the Big Gorilla

The Big Gorilla is that singular client, customer, vendor, or product on which you are heavily reliant. If it involves 25 percent or more of some part of your business (sales, vendors, customers) then consider it your Big Gorilla. For instance, if you have one great client who regularly orders what amounts to 25 percent of your monthly sales, you should think long and hard about the nature of your relationship with that customer. Obviously, before that client, 100 percent of your sales did not include that client, and when he first came along he seemed to be a very exciting acquisition. It seemed like you had 100 percent of your regular sales plus this new client who added 30 percent to that. Great! But as time wore on, you became accustomed to that client's order, and your sales volume and assessments included his order in your 100 percent of monthly sales. You likely adjusted your business based on his order, increasing your manufacturing and distribution costs to accommodate his needs, keeping more inventory on hand for him, or renegotiating other aspects of your business based on the volume he was allowing you to do.

Proceed with caution! The degree of dependence you now have on a force outside of your control should concern you. What if something happens to this client? Perhaps he is mismanaging his business in ways that you can't and don't see; perhaps when he dies a change in leadership will result in a change of his company's direction that does not include you; perhaps there is an as-of-yet undetected fraud at his business that will cripple his operations, not only preventing him from continuing to do business with you, but stalling his payments for a few months before your receivables department catches on and requests payment before future shipments. Let's consider the implications of that last possibility.

At Giant Manufacturing, one of our largest customers was paying its bill every sixty days, which was creating detrimental cash-flow problems. At its own behest, this customer slowed its payments down to ninety days. One of our central jobs became a restructuring of this client's contract and terms to ensure that if it faced problems, we would minimize the damage caused. Consider how much business that singular Big Gorilla is giving you. That's a great effect on your bottom line. However, the corollary is that this Big Gorilla is most likely to have the reverse impact, like obliterating a month's worth of your business.

Your Big Gorilla may not be in the form of a customer/client. It may be a product on which you are highly dependent. Or it may be a vendor who supplies most of your product line. One of my favorite Big Gorilla examples is the discount mart.

Awhile back I took over as the CEO of a manufacturing company that produced logo T-shirts and sweatshirts. The company did quality, steady work, and one day the discount mart started placing huge regular orders. The discount mart was most welcome as its business resulted in a capital infusion that allowed the company to grow its operation by leaps and bounds. In fact, the discount mart asked the CEO to change his manufacturing capabilities to suit its needs. Considering the business this giant was offering, how could he refuse? They were the discount mart, and they wanted to do a ton of business with this T-shirt company. So, of course, the CEO spent millions of dollars revamping the company's manufacturing capabilities based on the discount mart's requests. Printing on shirts can be done in a few different ways, and depending on the volume and colors needed for the shirts, different machinery is required. For the discount mart's T-shirt needs, the company upgraded its factory and equipment so that it could print at the volume the discount mart required and in as many colors as it needed. The upgrades were expensive, but they were for the discount mart. The orders were coming in, the profit line was increasing, and with this big customer in its corner, the company believed in the promise of much more business to come.

One day, after producing a million dollars worth of merchandise branded explicitly for the discount mart, this Big Gorilla told the CEO not to ship its order. The titan's sales were decreasing and the discount mart was managing its inventory levels. Considering it was a million dollar order with a cost basis of 60 percent, the discount mart certainly was acting nonchalant, and it was in this moment that the CEO felt the powerful punch of the Big Gorilla. This is the kind of influence that any Big Gorilla wields over its subject, and the CEO realized that he had a crisis and brought me in to help. I explained to him that he was lucky to still have all of the merchandise in his possession. At least with these T-shirts in hand we could brainstorm ways to cut his losses.

That's when the Big Gorilla really started to beat his chest. I believed that I could find a third-party market that would be interested in all of our overstock. I would have to sell the T-shirts at a steep discount and perhaps internationally, but at least I wouldn't let this company go into the red. After all, we couldn't reasonably sit on a million dollars worth of merchandise. It would be damaging to more than just the business's cash flow, which is one of the reasons I was brought in in the first place. But, "Oh no," said the discount mart. "You cannot sell the merchandise to anyone else; you have to destroy the T-shirts." So, not only did the discount mart not want the merchandise, it didn't want anyone else to have it. If we didn't comply, they said, they would never do business with our company again. Considering the upgrades we had gone through to accommodate its needs and the extreme lengths we had gone to in order for it to be happy, we couldn't believe this was happening. This CEO had fallen in love with the customer, and now the Big Gorilla really had him.

While corporate said to destroy, the purchasing agent, with a wink and a nod, suggested we sell in markets where the discount mart doesn't compete. So we decided to take our chances and seek out overseas markets that might be willing to buy the merchandise for fifty cents on the dollar. This is the kind of contingency plan I referred to in earlier chapters. If something happens and you can't move as much merchandise as you expected to, what are you going to do with that merchandise? How can you turn your merchandise into any amount of cash, which in a cash crisis is almost always more valuable than the merchandise itself? So we sought out overseas markets, and ultimately sold the million dollars worth of merchandise in South America for enough to cover our costs. We hadn't turned any kind of profit, but at least our warehouse wasn't overstocked and we were no longer sitting on worthless merchandise. Plus, this CEO had learned a valuable lesson about the power of the Big Gorilla.

We would have succeeded with it if a discount mart executive's son hadn't been vacationing in South America and purchased a souvenir for his father. The odds were slim, but we always knew the risk and evaluated it along with our decision to sell the merchandise. We figured better to sell something now than to bank on the misplaced promises of future business with the discount mart. After all, we had no idea if the discount mart would ever be able to continue our business relationship if it couldn't afford the merchandise it was already ordering. When the discount mart executive saw the souvenir, he terminated the discount mart's relationship with our company, which was a blessing and a curse: the Curse of the Big Gorilla.

I want you to learn from this CEO's experience with his Big Gorilla and be wary of your own. It's nice to land a big account, but when someone controls that much of your business, you have to be especially proactive, taking the kinds of precautions that will protect you and your company from the volatility that comes with dealing with a Big Gorilla. How? Start by assessing the relationship more carefully. Rather than following your inclination to extend even more grateful and special terms to this client, perhaps those terms should be stricter or backed by letters of credit. If his payment is even fourteen days late, you should make sure never to ship out a second month's order without inquiring into the matter and receiving payment. Have special discussions with your accounts receivable, and set special alerts on the Big Gorilla's account. Even better, consider diluting the percentage of your business that the Big Gorilla accounts for by learning more about the business and seeking out other comparable clients. Out of courtesy you may want to consider ones that don't compete in his direct market, as there's no better way to diminish his ability to pay you on time than by arming his competitors.

The Big Gorilla teaches us a valuable lesson in change. Change is the only constant in business. You can never expect anything to stay the same forever—and you can count on that. Your biggest client today can be your biggest gorilla tomorrow, and there's only one path you can follow to pro- tect yourself: create checks and balances and develop contingency plans. It's hard to say, "Prepare for change, and know exactly what to do when change happens," but simply by being aware, never growing complacent, recognizing that all projections have holes and flawed assumptions, and being proactive rather than reactive, you can prepare for change and protect yourself against its ramifications, especially when those ramifications are the swinging fists of the powerfully armed Big Gorilla.

Don't Bet the Ranch

Did you know that top-notch bull sperm is worth in excess of $75,000 a gallon? This is something I know firsthand thanks to Fred, the CEO of a manufacturing company in Texas. To clarify, Fred owned a company that had nothing to do with bull sperm, and that was precisely the problem for Fred's business. Fred's hobby was breeding the perfect Brahman bull, and it was an all-consuming hobby that caused Fred to lose sight of the bigger picture. For some strange reason, Fred thought that breeding the perfect bull would be the next step in his career. So he put all of his time and energy into this hobby and none into the endeavor of actually saving his family's struggling business. Fred bet the ranch.

I've said it before and I'll say it again: Don't bet the ranch. Don't gamble everything you have going on one particular endeavor. You can't fall in love with an idea, just like you can't fall in love with one client. If Fred had been more concerned about getting busy with his business rather than his bull, he may have saved his company. Fred's hobby got in the way, and he stopped paying attention to the business. When the company fell behind in interest payments, the bank realized that Fred was distracted and neglecting his business; they defaulted him on his loans and brought me in to clean up this sticky situation.

The problem with betting the ranch is that if your gamble doesn't pay off—that is, if you don't wind up with the world's most perfect Brahman bull whose sperm will make you a lot more money than your business—then you'll have a worthless bull and piles of bills. Indeed, that's what was bequeathed to me. I had a mismanaged and neglected manufacturing company to deal with that was more than $500,000 behind in payments to the bank. It was losing clients due to maintenance issues that resulted in spoiled products and declining income. Since the company was heading towards bankruptcy and on the path to being sold, it was my job to recover as many assets for the bank as I could. I fired Fred's overpaid and useless family members and held an auction at which I sold off bull sperm and a piece of equipment for $75,000. Turns out Fred's hobby wasn't worthless.

The CEO of the pipe manufacturer who was obsessed with his new hydroplane racer design that I discussed in Chapter 2 bet the ranch on a hobby instead of focusing on his business.

I was once brought into an injected molding company in Toledo, OH, because the president sunk $2.5 million of the business's money into his pet project: making the perfect bottle cap. He effectively leveraged the entire company by borrowing against it to pursue this dream. He bet the ranch. He went all in. He came out with nothing. Think of betting the ranch like going all in playing Texas Hold 'Em No Limit poker. Sure, you can go all in, and you can win, doubling up your chips (or knocking out another player). But you could lose, too. And if you go all in and lose the hand, you're out—with nothing to show for your efforts. That's what betting the ranch is, and that's why you should avoid doing it. Betting the ranch is either the desperate last move of a struggling enterprise or the result of falling in love with the product, deal, or client. A look at the mistakes of past CEOs shows that the risk isn't often worth the reward because betting the ranch is distracting, all-consuming, and rarely about the bigger picture.

Pick a Plan and Stick to It

I find that another typical CEO mistake is the CEO who can't focus on any one aspect of his business such that he's constantly changing his opinion and trajectory, confusing himself and everyone around him. This is most likely to happen when CEOs are facing crises and unsure of what to do next. The heart of the problem is that some CEOs, when they're facing crises, become only as smart as the last person with whom they spoke. They cease being able to think for themselves, whether out of some misplaced hope of being able to pass the buck or because anything and everything sounds better than what they're doing. That is a tremendous problem when it's your job to be a leader, to establish a clear direction, and to march in one direction.

When I was retained by an apparel manufacturer, the president had been terminated for various well-deserved reasons, and what they had on their hands was a crisis of leadership. Unfortunately, the interim president kept changing the restructuring plan with every person to whom he spoke. He'd announce firings and closings almost daily, and then backtrack when someone objected, subsequently calling those he'd fired to tell them to disregard their pink slip. Back and forth he'd go like this, only spouting the last thing someone else said to him. Imagine the emotional roller coaster this created for the staff and personnel. And while their emotions were on a roller coaster their operational efficiency was waiting in a long line because no one had any idea what to do other than stand in the fast-pass line for another trip on the emotional coaster. The only smart thing that the interim president did in his short tenure without changing his mind was hire me—and he was terminated once a more permanent solution surfaced. In the process of restructuring, you generally get one plan with which to move forward. The situation you're facing during a crisis is stacked like a house of cards, and you don't want it to topple from excess movement. Learn from the mistake of that interim CEO, and don't only be as smart as the last guy you talked to.

Acting on everything you hear and are told is like knee jerking with information, a very common reaction of CEOs who are doomed to fail. Some CEOs feel compelled to immediately react and respond to information. They get a letter from the bank warning them about their loan payments and call right away. A government agency leaves a few messages about wanting to talk and before thinking anything through the CEO calls back and starts blathering on about compliance. A director of marketing shares that a competitor released an excellent new product and before evaluating the ramifications, the reactive CEO orders a price drop on his key widget. Knee-jerking CEOs, who are only as smart as the last person they talked to, fail to validate information from multiple sources and end up making a variety of mistakes. In the process, they burn their people and lose their trust and interest.

I was retained by a pipe manufacturing company and one of the executive officers told the CEO that they were going to lose a large customer. As the operations manager, he wanted to cut back on ordering raw materials. The CEO, rather than follow up with the customer himself, cut their ordering of raw materials to prepare for this seemingly inevitable decline in business. It turns out that this customer wasn't leaving, but when the pipe manufacturing company didn't have enough raw materials to fulfill the next order, the customer did have to seek the product elsewhere—and ultimately switched to another supplier. Had the CEO not knee-jerked to the words of his operations manager but sought to verify the information, he wouldn't have set this self-fulfilling prophecy in motion, his company wouldn't have lost this customer, and I would never have been brought in to salvage the situation.

The opposite of the CEO who is only as smart as the last person he talked to is the CEO who does absolutely nothing: the CEO who is a deer caught in the headlights. When there is an 18-wheeler barreling down on them going 80 miles per hour, you'd be amazed at how many CEOs and company leaders stare right at their impending doom in the midst of a crisis. They just freeze up and wait for the impending SMACK!

I became the president of an apparel company that had entered a crisis. In the midst of this crisis, the very time-sensitive catalog that directly generated 80 percent of the $65 million annual revenue within a 120-day period had to be printed and mailed. For this to happen we had to have $25,000—immediately. In a cash crisis, the CEO, worth a few million himself, wouldn't take $25,000 out of his own pocket to pay the postage. This $25,000 personal investment when there was no money anywhere else would have generated a projected $52 million in revenue. What made this a no-brainer was that if anything went wrong, the CEO was personally guaranteed on $40 million. He would have been totally wiped out had he defaulted, and all he had to do was stake $25,000—but he froze. I was brought in within hours of the deadline and convinced him to put up the cash. This was the first of many critical decisions amongst endemic problems, but thankfully, this incident established trust and a working relationship that led to a successful restructuring plan. I taught him how to keep moving in one solid and forethought direction and not to freeze up at every problem.

> **When facing a crisis, pick one logical and reasonable plan and stick with it. Align everyone and everything in your company towards this goal and for this plan.**

Learn from these CEOs' mistakes and neither hop sporadically between plans and ideas nor tense up and do nothing. When facing a crisis, pick one logical and reasonable plan and stick with it. Align everyone and everything in your company towards this goal and for this plan. That is keeping your eyes on the Big Picture, and that is the most surefire way of ensuring your success and the survival of your company.

Continue to Evolve

In order to stay relevant and continue to grow your business you must continue to evolve and diversify it. As I've already discussed, you have to stay ahead of change. Change is coming, some positive and some less so. What will define you as a CEO is the way you prepare for change and the way you preempt it. Don't keep selling the same old stuff. You can tell me that Apple keeps selling computers, but the evolution inherent to their line of computers—and the diversity they brought to their offerings with the iPod, iPhone, and iPad—is the kind of change that I encourage you to pursue in your own line of products. I can't even count the number of businesses I've been asked to fix, only to discover that they have a few widgets that account for the bulk of their revenue coming off of the assembly line, they've turned into commodities, and they haven't evolved in twenty years. It doesn't take a turnaround professional to tell you that this approach and strategy, if it can be called that, isn't going to cut it for long in business. Diversify.

Mid Tech Relay was having problems that went far beyond their un-evolved product line. The company had 50 percent of its business tied up selling relays for traffic lights. On the surface, that's a problem. What wasn't a problem is that they controlled 90 percent of the marketplace. When you control 90 percent of a marketplace and are having cash-flow problems, you need to raise your prices. And I did. I raised prices 25 percent, immediately making the business profitable. I sold it right away and let the next guy worry about the other problems. He would need to evolve the product line by adding new widgets and services, ensuring that those were relevant to the market and in accord with the brand, but those are key components of being a proactive leader and understanding the big picture.

In the interest of continued evolution, pitch new product ideas to your current client list. Offer a generous discount at the beginning if you want to move enough product to test its relevance. See what kinds of new clients you can attract with your new products, skills, widgets, or offerings. Perhaps these new clients also need some of the products and services you've always offered, but they would never have found you had you not evolved by adding new products and services. Consider your marketplace and what's happening there. You are never selling a product—you are fulfilling a need. Consider the related needs of those who come to you to fulfill that original need and never lose sight of how that need itself is evolving.

The answers to these questions are how you can be guided to the next evolution of your widget.

Evolution is a fascinating thing. When explaining evolution to children, we say that animals evolved for certain needs. For instance, giraffes grew taller in order to reach higher leaves. This, however, is not the way that evolution works. Evolution is based on random genetic mutations that happen by chance and proved advantageous. Giraffes didn't develop longer necks in order to better reach leaves higher up in the trees. Rather, the giraffes who had the random genetic mutation that made their necks longer were able to reach leaves higher up in the trees, and this access to a food source facing less competition gave them an advantage over their shorter-necked kin. They were able to survive longer and breed more, subsequently passing on their genetic mutation to a higher percentage of offspring that eventually made for more giraffes with longer and longer necks. True as that all is, that's not the whole story of evolution.

For a very long time, Darwin's theory, as summarized and explained above, was accepted in this fashion. In more recent years, scientists have discovered that some genetic mutations are an intentional response to a creature's environment and not merely a result of some random mutation that proved to be advantageous from a survival standpoint. Experiments were done with certain reptiles that had a particular knack for looking like their environments: not chameleons who change color as they move through changing landscapes, but reptiles born looking one way their whole lives, but whose look is that of their environment. Scientists learned that within two generations certain reptiles could look entirely different if the environment around them and their parents was changed. If they started life in a leafy and green environment and looked like green leaves but before breeding were moved into a brown and sandier environment then by the second generation of breeding the offspring looked like the brown and sandy environment. That is, intentional advantageous genetic mutations were occurring that were changing these reptiles' permanent physical characteristics; evolution was actually working the way kids first understand evolution rather than the way Darwin explained it. This does not mean that all creatures can cause purposeful genetic mutations, but it does mean that there are multiple ways that species evolve.

Only one of the animals I described has a proactive evolutionary approach: the reptile. I encourage you to make yourself and your business more like the reptiles than the giraffes. Something in these reptiles' genetic code recognized that the environment was changing, and they didn't wait for chance mutations to make themselves better suited to survival. They actively changed themselves to be better adapted to their surroundings. They evolved voluntarily because change was inevitable and survival was a must.

A company that sells seat belt extenders was selling this product alone—in one color and one length. When sales started to dwindle a bit, the company's CEO realized that she needed to evolve her product offerings if she were going to survive in her business environment. In addition to increasing advertising and streamlining processes to become more efficient, her company needed to add products to its mix. Not only did it diversify by including different colors and lengths to the seat belt extender choices—a great move and an easy way to evolve—but it also added a handful of related products, all of which were highly relevant to the existing market and clientele (for instance, seat belt adjusters, bags to hold the extenders, etc.). Your evolution doesn't have to be complicated, and it doesn't have to cost you a lot. Instead of thinking about what you're already doing well, think about what you don't do well and bring in the people with the skills or the products and services that will evolve your business and round out its offerings.

Don't Fall in Love with the Deal

If it's too good to be true, well you know the rest of the saying. Part of business is making deals, and in the same way that I've encouraged you not to fall in love with a singular client, vendor, product, or hobby, I want to make sure that you don't fall in love with the deal. No deal is so sweet that it can't turn sour.

Have you ever bought a company before, or do you know anyone who's ever bought a company? If so, you might already be aware of this important fact, but I've had more than my fair share of turnarounds based on the mismanagement of purchasing another company. All companies have assets, and if you choose to purchase a company, make sure that you are actually only purchasing a list of its assets, rather than the stock of the company. The reason is simple: liabilities. All companies also have liabilities—known and unknown—particularly lawsuits and liability claims against them, to name but a few. If you're buying a business, and instead of purchasing the assets you buy the stock of that business then you as the shareholder or new owner also take possession of the liability and whatever else comes along in the meantime. That is why you only buy the assets of a business and not its stock because the assets do not come with liabilities, whether known or unknown. Buy the inventory, assume the real estate lease, buy the equipment, buy the license to use the brand and the name—buy all of the assets but do not buy the stock of a company.

I once found myself involved with a construction company that was facing a very rapid sale, which resulted in the buyer having to close the deal before the end of the year for tax reasons. Unfortunately, this hurried approach, while initially nice on his wallet, ultimately turned out to be to his detriment. What he discovered after the deal had closed was that there were some soon-to-be-discovered faults in the construction projects. As a result, the construction company went out of business, and the new owner lost everything in six months. Moreover, there was an environmental issue that arose due to some lead paint and diesel fuel that had been improperly dumped, and now the owner was on the hook for that problem as well. Had he slowed down rather than getting so caught up with the amazing deal that was falling into his lap then he would have taken the necessary time to consult with a competent lawyer who quite likely would have advised him to purchase the assets of the construction company rather than the whole company. He would never have lost anything because he would never have been on the hook for all of the problems that existed before he took over as CEO.

There can be reasons to buy the stock of a company, like certain licensing issues, but you have to be smart when you do it and build in reserves and a liability escrow for a certain amount of time to keep you from being faulted and having to shell out additional funds for issues that were in place before you arrived. A liability escrow will ensure that the seller doesn't receive all of the money for the business immediately so that some amount of the negotiated purchase price can go to covering you and the company in the event that something went undisclosed or undiscovered until after the deal was completed. Environmental Insurance, or other insurances relevant to the industry, should also be considered.

See the Forest Through the Trees

The impact of the Big Gorilla is felt as a result of being shortsighted, of not being able to see the forest through the trees. The important concept here boils down to one point: CEOs should not lose sight of the bigger picture even though the bigger picture is comprised of so many smaller components. I think a story about a mobile office will best illustrate this principle.

I often serve as a receiver, a court-appointed representative brought in to manage a company in a fiscally responsible way so that matters are properly reported and handled and creditors are provided with an accurate accounting of everything. What makes a case require a federal receivership rather than merely a state receivership is when the company has operations in more than one state. Towards the end of one dramatic case at which I was serving as a federal receiver, the company had overcome most of its issues and problems—including scaling back the operations, collecting receivables, and selling fixed assets—and it was starting to wind down the whole process by selling the plant through a court-approved Asset Purchase Agreement (APA). But that's when a $3,000 mobile office (a mobile home but with office furniture inside) got in the way of selling a $15 million piece of property.

It turns out that there was a tiny modular office sitting on one smidgeon of a sizable piece of property—one of three pieces of property that we were trying to sell. The mobile office had been used in one of the locations for a short period of time. As it happens, and unbeknownst to me until this very day, in that state one cannot—I repeat, cannot—sell a modular office without a title, similar to an automobile title. In our case the former business owner was not sufficiently cooperative and simply wouldn't get us the necessary title. (He was actually robbing the company blind and lying to me left and right—I uncovered hundreds of thousands of dollars of fraud in my first week there and gave him the boot. Needless to say he wasn't that interested in cooperating.) As a result of this minor inconvenience, the title company's lawyers were questioning the transaction that would have brought this extensive process to a close. For us to acquire a duplicate title through the proper government agencies would have taken an extra thirty-day extension to the closing date. This receivership had been long and arduous, and the victory close at hand was hard fought. No one wanted an extra thirty-day period to intervene before the closing date because who knew what alternate troubles could have arisen in that time.

This left me with an issue: the title company would not close the real estate transaction and the sale of the plant equipment without this last piece of the puzzle. To put that into a bit more perspective, I'm trying to sell a $15 million manufacturing plant, and I have a $3,000 modular office sitting on a far-off corner of it preventing the entire transaction because I don't have a piece of paper that says I can sell it—even though it's on my property and obviously mine. I only even begin to learn about this when the title company's lawyers call me, and not being as familiar as they with the nuances of state law as it pertains to modular property, I asked them to slow down and explain the problem in detail. This was after they and the buyer's lawyers convened on a conference call that cost us all $900 discussing a problem of seemingly equal value that was standing in the way of our $15 million deal.

I considered the matter myself and suggested that we just remove the modular home from the Asset Purchase Agreement. That meant we were selling one giant piece of property with manufacturing plants and equipment but the modular office sitting on it would continue to sit there, effectively having no owner and unattended. The title company lawyers objected on the grounds that the personal property taxes on the modular home were many years past due and were going to have to be covered and paid in full to close the sale because in a transaction in that state you have to pay all the past due personal property and real estate taxes. Well, at least now only $100 in taxes was holding up our $15 million sale. I suggested that we pay the tax on the modular home ourselves but remove the modular home from the APA and reduce the selling price accordingly. This made the title company's lawyers happy, and allowed us to move forward and close the sale. One more objection, though: would the buyer possibly agree to this deal without the modular office that would be sitting on his property? I called him and in forty-five seconds he agreed to the whole thing. Why? Because he had the larger deal in sight and refused to get hung up on a singular item.

This case is one of not seeing the forest through the trees, and it nicely summarizes the entire point of this chapter. As a successful CEO you must keep your eyes on the big picture. You must see the forest through the trees. There is always a way to work out every deal, but you will rarely find it if you can't keep the bigger picture in mind. When you find yourself confronted with a seemingly insurmountable detail always try to remember why you're doing what you do in the first place. In one way or another every aspect of this chapter represents a similar problem. Each issue raised is about not being able to understand, respect, or handle the larger operation of a business in light of the smaller challenges that face it. The positive aspects of the Big Gorilla blind us to the damage that he could inflict on our business

Your evolution doesn't have to be complicated, and it doesn't have to cost you a lot. Instead of thinking about what you're already doing well, think about what you don't do well and bring in the people with the skills or the products and services that will evolve your business and round out its offerings.

when inevitable change comes; crisis makes us as smart as the last person we spoke to or freeze like a deer in the headlights. All the same, we have to voluntarily evolve ourselves and our businesses to adapt to a constantly changing business environment in good times and bad if we want to grow and succeed.

Chapter 7

Keys to Success:
Buy-in & Communication

You are the leader of your business, but your business does not run by you alone. Each person in your business is responsible for a set of tasks or responsibilities, and those responsibilities are often better completed if their performer understands the larger context in which he is supposed to be executing them. The quality and efficiency of completion is enhanced even further when that person moves from a state of understanding to consent and even agreement—and that is buy-in.

Buy-in starts with communication, a topic that we've already visited on a few occasions, most notably the 10 C's of Bank Relationships for CEOs. I hope by now you believe me when I emphasize how important it is that you communicate fully and regularly with your banker, especially when you are experiencing some kind of financial or cash-flow crisis, as each of those problems affects his bank's money. Your banker, however, is not the only person in your business life who deserves and needs open communication if you're not to make the same mistakes as many failed CEOs.

Honest and open communication goes a long way. People try to lead without input, and that rarely works. Leaders do run businesses—not committees—but if leaders are honest with those involved, especially key stakeholders like boards, banks, creditors, and management teams, then there is a much greater chance for success. Let's explore the reasons and values behind open and honest communication, trust building, an open door policy, and buy-in.

Establish An Open Door Policy

People need to believe that you, as their leader, are there for them to talk to. It's not necessarily that you are meant to be a place for general grieving and gripes—though an anonymous suggestion box can be quite advantageous—but you should be available to speak with your employees when their best judgment and discretion guide them to you. There is an episode of a television show in which a large company is taken over by a new parent company. The president of this large company is an old school, conservative, dictate-from-the-top-down kind of leader. The CEO of the new parent company instructs him, contrary to his inclinations, to spend a whole day each month listening to every single person in the organization who wants to share an idea, no matter how big or small their position or outlandish their thoughts. The president of this company would never have dreamed of opening his door to common employees and is horrified at the notion, yet at the same time, the greatest idea he hears—and steals—is from one of the company's lowliest employees.

My suggestion is that you find some kind of happy medium between the president's initial management style and the regular idea sharing days that he was forced to endure. As a CEO, it's important to know which direction you want to head, since your business is not a voting democracy and you're its leader for a good reason; at the same time, you

> **You never know where some of the best ideas are going to come from until you commit to an open door policy.**

shouldn't just be handing down dictates from on high. People need to feel like they have access to you in the event that they really need it, and they need to feel comfortable speaking with you, whether they have an idea or a complaint. You never know where some of the best ideas are going to come from until you commit to an open door policy.

One of the biggest problems I notice when I go into troubled companies is that CEOs have created an environment of borderline fascism in which people are terrified to share what they know for fear that they are going to be considered guilty by association or punished for some kind of imagined insolence. This kind of corporate culture won't get you or your business very far, which is why your employees need to feel comfortable approaching you with anything. If your company is small enough—say, under thirty employees—you could schedule a bi-annual meeting with all employees to ensure their happiness, that they have everything needed to complete their jobs, and that they are able to share any of their ideas. When company size makes that impractical, these meetings could move to your department heads as the company grows, and people could still reserve the right to request that their meeting be conducted with you. The goal here is to ensure that everyone feels comfortable speaking to management and sharing what he feels needs to be shared.

The first thing I do when I get into a company is to cultivate an open door policy. I find that it's one of the best ways to discover fraud that had otherwise gone undetected. It's rare that fraud is being perpetrated and that someone else doesn't know or suspect something—and is perturbed by it—but the problem is that there's rarely a channel through which an employee can safely go to report the fraud he's discovered, and he doesn't know if he can trust the person to whom he reports it. That's why I conducted that midnight barbecue. I had no idea that it was going to result in the uncovering of a multi-million dollar fraud, but I was seeking to establish an open door policy—a feeling of camaraderie and communication that conveyed to people that they could talk to me.

My strategy at a new out-of-town company is to ask publicly what good restaurants are near my hotel. In that way, I inform everyone where I'm staying, so that they can share information with me without others knowing they're doing so (and potentially to protect their own anonymity if that remains a fear). At one company I assured the staff that no one would lose his job for sharing information, asked them all about where to eat, and went back to my hotel. In the middle of the night someone shoved a fistful of USB drives under my door filled with data and files that effectively explained where all of the company's money had gone. That's not the first time that happened. I've also had paper files and documents shoved under my door in the middle of the night with plenty of valuable information. In order to share this kind of information, though, people not only have to trust you, but they have to believe that you will do something important with the information they give you. That is going all the way on your open door policy. You can't invite employees into your office and then belittle them after they share an idea with you.

On another occasion an open door policy saved me a quarter million dollars. Retama Park was a horseracing track I turned around. It cost $100 million and eighteen months to build—and thirty days for it to run out of working capital. In fact, Retama Park represents one of the fastest descents I've ever been brought in to fix. I was interviewed for the job along with a handful of other turnaround professionals, all of whom had extensive experience with horses and horse racing in some capacity or another. Believing that an open and honest approach was best, I told the owners of Retama Park that I didn't even know which end of a horse to get on, but obviously knowing about horse racing hadn't worked for their business anyway. Like I mentioned earlier about doctors and other professionals, it's important to do what you do best and at some point let business people handle the jobs that they do best. Perhaps, I told the owners of Retama Park, what they needed was a fresh perspective. Part of my fresh perspective was soliciting more buy-in from the people who'd been a part of building the horse racing track but who didn't seem to have a great degree of communication with the central management.

There was a big lake in the middle of the racetrack, and when I arrived the lake was empty. An empty lake is actually just a big muddy hole. As it happens, those good folks had already spent a quarter million dollars building themselves this glorified muddy hole. They'd filled the lake up with millions of gallons of water, and unfortunately, it all leaked out. That's an incredible amount of wasted water, and a quarter million dollars down the drain is nothing to scoff at either. When I asked why they couldn't just leave the big muddy hole empty, they explained that during simulcast and live racing, our track was broadcast into every betting parlor in the country, and a muddy hole made our track look terrible. Nobody wanted to look at a track that had a big, empty, muddy hole in the middle of it. Reasonable enough, I agreed. We needed to fill up the lake.

One engineer stated that the lakebed was fine and we could use city water to fill up the lake again. He prepared to do just that, and boy, was it a good thing I had my open door policy in place. Just as he was on his way to fill up the lake, Randy came sheepishly into my office. He seemed pretty scared at the notion of sharing his opinions with upper management (not the environment that should have been cultivated), but he had come because I said that I was here to listen to everyone—that everyone's ideas mattered. Realizing that I was sincere, Randy told me that if I filled the lake up, all the water would leak out again. He said the wrong type of clay had been used on the base of the lake, and that was the problem we'd been having. At this point I had two people with a difference of opinion, so I stopped the lake from being filled and brought in an engineering firm to assess the situation. The engineers confirmed Randy's assertion: the base had been laid incorrectly, and we'd need to redo it—for a half million dollars. If I hadn't exercised my open door policy and conveyed to Randy that I really wanted to know what he had to say, he would never have felt comfortable enough coming to my office and advise me not to fill up the lake again. I didn't want to spend a half million dollars redoing the lake, but I was much happier not wasting a quarter million dollars filling it up a second time, only to find myself with the same big muddy hole needing a half million in repairs and then a quarter million fill up.

Another instance in which an open door policy was crucial was the widget business I consulted to in Massachusetts. I was brought in to restructure a manufacturing plant there that made widgets for guided missiles. The company was steadily running three shifts to produce the necessary parts, but for some reason the cost of goods was going up while the prices remained steady. We couldn't figure out why or where the profit was going, but something was definitely wrong. Fortunately, somebody came to me, again because of my open door policy, and shared with me that there was a new competitor that had bid on a government contract, and the government had awarded that company 25 percent of its widget needs. Well, that explained where some of our business was going, but it didn't explain the rise in our cost of goods. Apparently, the nightshift manager on the third shift was a silent partner in this other company, and as it happens he was stealing from our widget company and giving the "scraps" to his other company. He could compete on the government bids because his materials were free and our costs were rising since a higher percentage of our supplies were being written off as scrap.

An anonymous suggestion box is also a helpful tool. Like the open door policy, the most important part of the suggestion box is that, as the CEO, you have to be willing to read the suggestions and listen to them. If a suggestion box is what it takes to get your employees to know that you're listening, then I highly suggest you put one up. You could even set up an email box like suggestions@yourcompany.com and make the password something public. Anyone could then log into this account and write you an anonymous email.

When I go into companies at which the CEO or president hasn't been listening to anyone, I know that's been to his detriment and that it's a challenge I will have to overcome. Good communication up and down an organization will alert you to myriad ways that you could be improving your company.

A final advantage to a suggestion box and open door policy is that they're superb ways to canvas your organization for quality and overlooked talent. Much as you might like some of your directors and managers, your business is your business and their jobs are their jobs. You act in the best interest of your business, yet they might be acting in the best interest of their jobs, and that can mean not noticing talent that could one day overtake them and their positions. When I have to rebuild an organization that's been ravaged by fraud or poor management or lay-offs, I always need a new management team, and there are often great people on the inside with a profound understanding of the organization. If you are in upper management, utilize the talent beneath you. Listen to people. Don't overlook their suggestions. Employees often know the solutions to turning around a company but are ignored. Generally I act as a catalyst and implement a lot of their suggestions. One of the key markers of a successful company is that it's a place where all employees are heard. It is very demotivating to be an employee and to know that you have no voice. A lot of CEOs lost their companies by not listening, and I hope that you'll let an open door policy raise you to new heights of success.

Get Buy-in

There is nothing quite so important in leadership as buy-in, as knowing that those who you are directing are listening to what you want done and that they're on board and prepared to make it happen with you. Getting buy-in, in part, is about earning people's trust. People aren't going to agree to follow a general into battle who they do not trust. That's not to say that you won't get people to do what you want by motivating them with money or fear, but in my experience, and in the experience of the many failed CEOs whose messes I've cleaned up over the years, building trust and getting buy-in is a much easier, more ethically luminous and successful way to go.

When I first arrived at the electronic parts manufacturer in El Paso, TX, (home of the Dragon Lady of El Paso, you might recall), I earned people's trust when I supplied toilet paper and coffee, "compliments of Lee." From then on, they loved me. I had full buy-in, no one lost his job and we sold the company in full six months later. My basic gesture of humanity and understanding—after all, coffee and toilet paper are essentials—immediately established trust; word spread, and people were prepared to buy-in to my model for how to get their company turned around and operational again.

The cheerleaders at Cheerleader Supply were also part of teaching me this valuable lesson of buy-in very early in my career. Every member of the staff and board wanted Cheerleader Supply to succeed and see its way through Chapter 11 bankruptcy. The judge wanted us to succeed. The lawyers and bankers wanted us to succeed. It's a pretty coldhearted villain who doesn't want a cheerleading company that trains boys and girls at cheerleading camp to succeed in emerging from bankruptcy. As I looked around from the helm of this organization at all of these people who were following my lead (though if only they knew how much I was following theirs at the time) and buying into my plan because I was communicating with them openly and honestly about what we were going to do and how we were going to do it and soliciting their thoughts and feedback in the meantime, I knew that the power of buy-in was one of the most important forces in leadership. The many miserable, failed CEOs who I watched make the mistake of squandering trust, communication, and buy-in during subsequent turnarounds reinforced the reality of this truth.

Though monetary incentives are not often a great way to motivate people with buy-in, they can be an excellent reward for people buying-in and communicating and becoming part of the solution rather than the problem. I became the most popular guy in town, after convincing the private capital firm that was the investor in the seminar company in Chapter 1 to let me give 20 percent of the next year's net profit to the thirty-five guys who made the restructuring happen (and we did $4 million that next year!). They were all from inside the company, and they all stepped up when I encouraged them to buy-in to this process of restructuring. I told them that it was not going to be The Lee Show and that it was going to be their chance to fix their broken company and have their thoughts and ideas heard and executed. They generated 95 percent of the great ideas that fixed the company, and I was merely the catalyst for that process. The company had an $8 million swing in one year, going from a negative $4 million to $4 million in profit. Without getting their buy-in and convincing them to communicate with me, I could never have learned about and implemented their great ideas, and we never would have wound up with one of the most rapid and successful turnarounds of all time. You already know that Larry at the seminar company wouldn't listen to a word anyone else had to say, and you can see now how starkly that proved to his detriment. The answers to his debt and cash flow problems were sitting all around him as he plugged his ears: they were his staff. All I did was step into his place and listen to them.

Communicate Openly and Regularly

Companies—like militaries, countries, families, and people—face hard times. As your company's leader, it's your job to get everybody through the hard times and ensure that they are prepared to see the good ones again. If you go through a rough patch at your business and the employees and staff resent you for those challenges because they didn't know what was happening, then they may cease to fully contribute, leave, cripple your company, and make you conclude that you shouldn't have spent money on a turnaround in the first place. If that was your approach, you should have resigned to call it a day and get on with your life because everyone else will have, too. On the contrary, it's best that staff understand what's happening and why. Open communication and buy-in will steer your company through hard times.

"Chainsaw" Al Dunlap was a workout guy whose methods were a little different from mine. In his day he had a tremendous success rate for creating shareholder value; however, the Sunbeam-Oster Corporation assignment was his Waterloo and the company subsequently filed for bankruptcy. His goal was not to create a better class of CEOs and business leaders but to stop a business from failing—period. He would go into companies, slicing and dicing, laying people off, cutting product lines, and selling off assets as fast as he could. As his name suggests, he took the chainsaw approach. Chainsaw was a pro at Turnaround 101, but he did it with little finesse. As you might imagine, after the slash and burn lay-offs and fire sales, there's still a company at which you don't want everyone to be demoralized and miserable. Chainsaw did not believe in communication beyond the pink slip, nor did he leverage the concept of buy-in.

In contrast to Mr. Chainsaw, I always make an effort to educate a company's personnel throughout the process of a turnaround and solicit their buy-in for what I'm doing. Like I said, I didn't turn around the seminar company myself. I used the team that Larry already had in place but refused to utilize. The company desperately needed to be turned around, but the Chainsaw approach would have meant hacking off limbs, when instead all that we really needed was to listen to some good ideas from people on the inside and solicit their feedback and buy-in for what we were doing. This kind of communication doesn't just need to happen during a turnaround, though; it should happen all the time.

Regularly sit down with your team members so that they understand your solutions and decisions. I'm not suggesting that your team gets to vote and potentially overturn your ruling—a business is not, I reiterate, a democracy—but you do need to communicate about big ideas. As a side note, if you do take a vote just out of curiosity and find that 67 percent of your key team would otherwise vote against your ideas, you might want to reconsider your approach or at least the ramifications of your approach. If you think they're all foolish for opposing you then reconsider who you're hiring. There is some kind of disconnect in a situation like this, and it's your job as the CEO to figure out what it is and to realign everyone in the best interests of the company.

> **Regularly sit down with your team members so that they understand your solutions and decisions.**

The reason you need this kind of buy-in is because, as the president of your company, it's unlikely that you're out there day to day screwing on the wheels of a car, fixing machinery, drawing up marketing designs and product containers, bolting your widget together, etc. That means that if everyone disagrees with your approach, you don't have the reach to assuage the negative feelings running through the veins of your company—and you won't even know about them. I'm not suggesting that they'll outright sabotage your operations, but a lack of motivation and interest can cause people to work slower, make more mistakes due to basic negligence, and ignore the requests and instructions of their supervisors. When you achieve the buy-in of your team members and allow them to understand what you're doing and why—even if they don't agree with every move you make—they will help educate the survivors of the turnaround process to know that they're going to be better off after the turnaround. This also applies to healthy companies.

I was taking my son to school years ago, and he asked me, "What are you doing today?" I told him that I had a rough day ahead of me because I was going to Philadelphia to lay off 200 people and close a division of a company. He looked at me like I was an ogre and asked how the kids of those laid-off parents would be able to afford camp, get baseball gloves, and enjoy candy (now with kids of his own his concerns still lie in these three areas). I told him that by laying off 200 people and closing one plant, I was saving 600 jobs and keeping the company alive. Certainly what I had to do was terrible for some people, but it was for the greater good. If I didn't let 200 people go today then I'd have to let 800 go next month. In a turnaround or crisis at your company, your challenge as the CEO is not to bemoan those 200 people; it's to ensure that the 600 remaining employees are reenergized, reengaged, and brought into the process of what comes next. That's the real challenge of a turnaround, and that is why you must communicate and get buy-in for the process.

The apparel manufacturer I mentioned in Chapter 6 was a case where communication acted as the glue that brought the turnaround together. It was only through extensive meetings that we earned the support to proceed with our forbearance agreement, and that is what gave us time to hire a new president and to show results from our efforts. We had to be very open about our designs and plans and consistently honest about what was happening, and even when things didn't go exactly as hoped, it was our regular communication that convinced creditors and others to allow us to continue on our path. This kind of buy-in was contagious up and down the organization, and this spirit amongst the staff contributed immensely because people felt they were a part of the turnaround. They were committed to the company and seeing it survive. Anything I needed from them I got. Being part of a team that believes in the cause is a great thing, and in a crisis it's essential to return to core values and purpose and to lean on them and the team.

Don't Burn People

Even though some CEOs seek no buy-in whatsoever, those who recognize the value of information often communicate with people around their companies to learn whatever they can and to use that information for the betterment of their businesses. In a turnaround, this kind of fact-finding is an essential part of the process, and one of the most valuable lessons I can convey about it is ensuring that you do not burn your sources. Nothing eviscerates trust like burning those who give you valuable intelligence.

At a national mortgage company I was doing an assessment prior to becoming the director of reorganization. Before I had even begun my job, the president decided to burn me, because he thought it would ruin my credibility and keep me out of his hair. When I started the assessment the chairman of the board gave me specific people with whom to discuss certain issues, and before I arrived at each of these meetings my credibility had long since been torched. The president had told senior staff members that I had made up my mind about what I was going to do in relation to a restructuring of their divisions. Of course I had not, because if I had made up my mind then I would never have bothered talking to them—why waste everyone's time like that? As I've just outlined, I always speak with people at a company first to communicate openly and honestly and start achieving the buy-in that I know I'll need later. Nonetheless, he chose to burn me to his people, and that hurt my credibility and ruined my hopes of successful and open communication. His ship was sinking, and he was determined to direct it all the way into the depths of the ocean. I wasn't about to let that happen, though.

The president of the mortgage division who was on the executive team came to me and supplied me with a list of issues regarding other divisions within the company. His hope was that I would focus on these issues instead of wasting time on the diversionary tactics of other division managers—and his boss. As most people do, he had his own agenda, but his suggestions were a concrete step in the right direction and proved integral. My challenge then became not to burn him as I'd been burned. I had to continue taking deliberate steps in a particular direction, often with a great deal of knowledge about the surrounding conditions, but without revealing the source of my information. I had to work backwards when asking what might otherwise have seemed like pointed questions.

Had I burned my source he would have become the most hated and maligned person at the mortgage company, and his career there would have been over. Most of what he told me, though, was correct and important, and I needed his help to do my job as successfully as I did. This president of the mortgage division became part of the restructuring team solely because I didn't burn him as a source when he told me what he knew, and that allowed people to continue working with him comfortably. Typically, senior people at a company will tell me that their subordinates will not open up to me out of either loyalty to management or fear of me and what I intend to do. In my experience, the opposite is true. People are so grateful to have a sympathetic ear that it's generally the employees who tell me what I need to know. After all, they see where the waste is occurring, and they have a general sense of what to fix—and how much their company needs turning around. In the process of earning their trust and encouraging people to open up to me, though, I have to be sure not to burn them. That's hardly a reward for their honesty; yet you'd be shocked at how many CEOs squander the knowledge that they've been given by divulging their sources.

Clarify with the Whiteboard

Many leaders can accept the general principle that they need to do a better job communicating, but they're not entirely sure how to start doing so in their day-to-day operations. What information do they share with employees and their management teams? How do they share it? In memos, public notification boards, or via bullhorns? In a 2,000-person organization I'm not proposing that the CEO become an open book for all to read. I don't want you to start blogging about senior staff meetings. First, consider those people with whom you need to communicate most regularly and fully. I've already emphasized that in crisis situations you need to communicate with the key stakeholders in your business: your board, creditors, banker, lawyer, etc. For larger projects, directions, and planning, I suggest that you continue to involve your board, your directors, and your key management team, as well as anyone else whose buy-in would be particularly important and whose input could make a difference.

The whiteboard is an excellent tool by which to communicate. Many a company has found itself turned around by going through the whiteboard exercise with key personnel precisely because it is an excellent way to communicate and achieve buy-in. A whiteboard lends clarity to complex situations and helps viewers logically analyze the many issues surrounding a case or problem. The whiteboard also allows you (and others) to see the holes in your logic—and therefore solidify your case by dealing with those holes. Other whiteboard sessions reveal that you had the wrong fact in place, but that revelation will only occur if those people involved with a plan or process are present during the whiteboard exercise. Many times

> **Many a company has found itself turned around by going through the whiteboard exercise with key personnel precisely because it is an excellent way to communicate and achieve buy-in.**

I find that people are operating under the pretense of erroneous information, so when I make them share their thoughts on a whiteboard, they elucidate their wrong presumptions and correct them. In short, whiteboards get everyone on the same page, and that makes them an essential tool for communication. I find that timelines are one of the most useful ways to employ a whiteboard and achieve buy-in because people are confronted with the reality of their responsibilities in front of others, and so their consent is public rather than dictated. Pledging consent and buy-in to a group of peers is a far more effective means of ensuring compliance than handing down a dictate from above, because the former creates an environment of accountability through mutual agreement. Leverage that element of social dynamics by communicating openly with your team, rather than telling each person individually what you want him or her to do.

With one client we strategized a Chapter 11 bankruptcy case and created a timeline that included everything from the details of the date of filing to the date of exiting, thinking the whole process would take nine months. As we made the timeline we assigned specific tasks and responsibilities to people, and we also added our goals. By placing our goals at appropriate time intervals and getting buy-in from everyone involved, each person could see how missed deadlines would affect everyone else's timing throughout the process. When I use the whiteboard for bankruptcy planning, the process works beautifully because everyone is in the room as people agree that they have enough time to do their jobs according to the timeline. The pressure of accountability that results from group consent also gives everyone the comfort to say when he does not believe that his responsibilities can be accomplished because he fears agreeing to something he knows would affect the entire team, process, and business so dramatically. That kind of honesty is extremely important, as you don't want buy-in to be forced. You want people to understand what's really being asked of them and by when, so that they can be an effective part of the plan and team. The whiteboard is an amazing way of creating that process visually.

I wanted to get Retama Park, the horse racing track, out of bankruptcy in eighteen months. With my initial filing I also needed marketing plans, PR, and other "why we'll survive" materials. There was an opening period to fine-tune operations for profitability and positive cash flow, restructure the bonds, and maintain a line of credit—and by day 450 we needed the disclosure statement hearing and approval so that in eighteen months we were out of bankruptcy. People said it couldn't be done—that is, I didn't have buy-in—but after putting the timeline on the whiteboard so that they could visualize the process, we were able to get the necessary buy-in by asking each person involved what he needed to complete his responsibilities on time. Without a whiteboard workout this turnaround never would have happened. Only by mapping everything out for all involved was I able to get buy-in and approval.

And whiteboard timelines aren't just for bankruptcies. They facilitate nearly any task: moving production lines, BK plans, relocating your offices, planning a wedding, or whatever else. With a timeline visualized on a whiteboard you can accomplish the all-important task of buy-in, understand milestones, and see how adjustments need to be made. The tool can be especially effective if you add a budget to your whiteboard timeline.

A case of whiteboard communication and buy-in that stands as a marquis example is the company in Florida (Company A) that bought a business in Minnesota (Company B) and wanted to move it to Florida and have it operational in three days. Recall that their plan was to shut down a factory in Minnesota, drive its equipment and operations to Orlando, set it back up in an inadequate space, train all the personnel in the new assembly process and be fully operational—without disrupting their supply line, output, customer service, or other operations—over the course of a holiday weekend.

The most glaring problem was that Company A had no inventory built up to handle orders if the production line didn't come up Monday morning as they expected it would. There was no contingency plan. Stockpiling inventory, therefore, was at the top of the priority list. In addition, the assembly line personnel in Orlando didn't understand how to operate the equipment that was being used in Minnesota. It wasn't so distant from their core competency, but it certainly required training and oversight. Company A planned to send one guy from Minnesota to Florida to teach people how to put their widget together in three hours. What if something happened to this guy? What if the entire crew didn't pick up on his instructions in a few hours? Finally, the capacity in the Florida location was full, and there was absolutely nowhere to put all of this new equipment or any time built into this plan to find a new location.

My biggest challenge was communicating to this team that their plan was absolutely impossible, but then I realized that my solution was all in the whiteboard. I asked someone who was pitching this implausible idea to come up to the whiteboard and sketch out a timeline. How was this process really going to happen? As these board members and management teams took the dry erase marker and their turn at sketching this process out publicly, factoring in equipment breakdown time, drive time and reassembly, each yelling at the one with the marker to put this here and that there, they quickly proved to themselves that not only did they have no idea how this was going to happen, but also that it simply could not happen. At this point, they gave me back the marker and prepared to listen to my solution.

I mapped out the process of moving and consolidating this business on the whiteboard as a two-month timeline. By doing this, I both identified all of the steps necessary and included everyone's responsibilities to make this happen efficiently and effectively. I solicited buy-in at each and every step to ensure that people knew what their responsibilities were, that they agreed to them, and that they saw what would happen to the plan if they didn't succeed. The primary goal of the first part of the timeline was to build up inventory, running overtime at the Minnesota plant (which was also very nice for all of those employees who were about to be laid off), so that when they closed the production line they had a full thirty days worth of inventory to get operational in Florida. In the meantime, the Orlando crew needed to be properly trained. I suggested that they send the factory workers in Orlando to Minnesota on a rotating schedule to watch the process there for a few days. Company A complained that they didn't have the time to do this, but if their plan didn't work they would have lost millions of dollars in sales, customers, time, and energy. Penny wise and pound foolish, if there was ever an example. With two months for this process to take place, there was now adequate time to find a suitable location at a reasonable price for the Minnesota factory to be relocated in Florida. Learn from past CEOs' mistakes and use the available tools at your disposal to get buy-in from key stakeholders.

Conclusion

Congratulations on graduating from Turnaround 101. I hope this crash course on how not to hire a guy like me was everything you needed. If you feel otherwise, I'm confident that at some point in your career—or maybe more than once—you'll find yourself saying, "Hmm, so that's what Lee was talking about." When that day comes, this book will have been just the forewarning you needed to ensure yourself safe passage to the next chapter of your business. Keep it close at hand.

I'm often asked in client interviews what my success rate is, and I submit to you that the answer is in the eyes of the beholder. Therefore, my success is based on my client's definition of success. If the CEO wanted to get off the hook for his company's debt, keep his assets and his home—and I've accomplished that—then I'm pleased. That measure puts me between 80 and 90 percent, but it's the other 10-20 percent of cases that should interest you because they're the ones that speak most directly to the need to involve a professional in business crises. In those remaining cases, "failure," in the eyes of the CEO, seems like a foregone conclusion when said CEO wants an outcome he can't have, due to the fact that he's kept the truth from me and is in some way committing fraud, self-dealing, aligning politically against me, or worse. Achieving a fair outcome for creditors, selling a business to keep jobs, or restructuring a company, in these cases, should be viewed as successes in their own rights.

I was turning around a white goods retailer in Louisiana. My initial assignment was to negotiate a forbearance agreement, renegotiate lease and supply contracts, and improve operations. In my initial interview the president/guarantor informed me that he had fifteen stores, two of which were guaranteed. In the first month on the job I learned that 90 percent of his leases were actually guaranteed, an enormous difference that affects strategy. On top of that, there was an additional million dollars of contractual obligations that was not on the books. Five months into this still successful turnaround, the president was sued out of left field by a contractor on a distribution center. When it rains it pours.

The president was lucky that I settled the suit for $250,000 within six weeks, even though that wasn't what he'd imagined as a success. Had information been communicated accurately, I would have steered the project in the right direction from the beginning. While these challenges come with the turnaround territory, they also bolster the necessity of involving a professional early on in a crisis; professionals dramatically change the odds of success, even if that success is not what a CEO had imagined. Without me or someone like me involved in a crisis like this one, the odds of failure would have been close to 100 percent, so a 90 percent chance of success with me is an enormous swing in the right direction.

> **Stress is perhaps the single largest impediment any CEO faces when it comes to having a successful turnaround.**

One of the reasons that I have the ability to succeed where CEOs faced by crises do not is because it is not my business. It's not my company, my employees, my money, my spouse, my family, or my life. That allows me to keep a clear head and an objective perspective where the CEO does not have one. Personal involvement compromises the CEO's ability to understand what's important and what is not; the facts and information that manifest themselves during an assessment and what ultimately resolves a turnaround are rarely the same facts and information that the CEO initially deemed relevant. That personal involvement creates conflict and leads me to the final piece of management advice I want to discuss: stress management.

Stress is perhaps the single largest impediment any CEO faces when it comes to having a successful turnaround, and I dare argue that it's poor stress management that lands many CEOs in crisis situations. We touched on this briefly when we talked about seeing the forest through the trees, but one technique we didn't discuss was how to achieve big picture perspective when you can't help but be mired in the daily grind. With any client and job, there are basics that I must do: assess the company, review the assets, increase the top line, slash expenses, liquidate assets, and strengthen key partnerships. A challenge underlying each of these necessities, though, is managing the CEO's stress, especially when there are surprises and when circumstances don't go as expected. Teaching CEOs how to manage the stresses in their lives is crucial to guiding them through a crisis, and in my experience, it's those who can't handle the stress who get left behind as one piece of the turnaround.

When I'm mired in a turnaround and politics cripple my progress, a weird aura creeps over my investigations, and the situation is less as it seemed upon the initial assessment, I need to extricate myself from my surroundings to reflect. For me, distance softens stress and attracts clarity. The lack of external influence and stimulus allows me to meditate on the pieces of the puzzle that comprise each turnaround. For me, this reflection occurs on a 30-mile bike ride, during a 90-minute massage, or throughout an afternoon on the beach (and sometimes all three). During this process, stress fades and my brain can start rearranging the puzzle pieces. It's in these passive activities that I find my ah-hah moment, that crucial detail or key decision that allows me to guide the turnaround in the right direction.

Learn to step back from the day to day such as the stresses of the job, your wife's distress at potentially losing her home, your employees' morale, your vendors' calls. It is in this distance that you will better be able to separate the signal from the noise, the wheat from the chaff, what is important from what is not.

Far too often I speak with CEOs who complain that they haven't been able to get away from the job for years. That should be a warning sign to you. Vacations are hugely important; aside from relaxation and preventing (or postponing) burnout, they provide a necessary distance that is essential to maintaining perspective. Without the pressure of daily stresses, we, as CEOs and business leaders, can better see where the correct path lies.

I had a client who took this advice to heart. He was getting beat up by a bankruptcy and worsening family issues. He couldn't get any perspective on his business or his life, so he decided to go on a one-month mission while his trusted second in command handled the business. He returned with a new attitude and unique solutions to his challenges and business problems. Everything he brought back with him wasn't solid or viable, but the distance and mind-clearing nature of his experience allowed him to gain the perspective that he needed. His renewed passion and ability to work on his business and towards its successful turnaround made him an excellent partner in the process of saving his company.

In part, it is caring about CEOs' personal stresses that separates me from other turnaround professionals. I've been accused of caring too much. It seems like a strange accusation, but it remains unconventional in my field.

I adopt a guardianship of you, your family, your employees, and your business. Your success is my success and your happiness is my happiness. It is not just about a paycheck for me. Saving businesses and those who work for them is how I create value for communities.

Being a successful CEO requires a diverse skill set, and inevitably, we can't all have the skills necessary to handle every aspect of running a company. A CEO skill set in one industry may not totally transfer to another industry; the CEO of a retailer may not make the transition to a manufacturer. Fortunately, many of us who try have enough of the skills needed to do a good job, and we recognize (if not before reading this book then hopefully now) that we can surround ourselves with those who have the talents and skills that we lack.

However, this book is not about having the skills needed to handle regular business. There are already numerous books about management, sales, marketing, and the like. This book is about what to do during crises, what actions—or inactions—are so often precursors to those crises, and how you, as the leader of your company, can be proactive enough to prevent those crises or handle them when they strike—and all without hiring a guy like me. I believe that you now have the knowledge to recognize the signs of an impending crisis before it occurs and the tools to take the actions necessary to steer your company through it.

Acknowledgements

I've had so much support through this long process and want to acknowledge those who may or may not know how much they've meant to me.

First and foremost, Jay Solomon and Eszter Boda for their support, writing and editing skills, and their love for this project. They helped me bring an idea to reality.

The gray-hair Grisanti, Galef & Goldress partners who evolved into the Musketeers, and to the GGG Partners for continuing the brand and professionalism.

Marv Davis for giving me my first workout assignment as CFO of a large construction company wrought with fraud. It was a great opportunity.

Jerry Goldress, for waiving his belief that nepotism has no place in the office. Yes, family businesses can succeed but it helps if one's offices are 2,500 miles apart.

Bud Carter, my Vistage International Chairman, who inspired and pushed me to write this book; and to my Vistage Group #150 for their insight, friendship and clarity of problem solving.

Jan Schroder, Editor and Publisher, for believing in the book and showing genuine amazement and wonder at the stories and solutions.

Donna Fleishman, my PR consultant and friend for her insights.

My sons, Sam and Randall, for their love and understanding; and to their sweet wives, Genifer and Erica.

Mark Solomon for his continued concern about my well-being.

The bankers, asset managers, lawyers, and accountants with whom I've worked over the many years. I appreciate your trust, support, and referrals.

The CEOs, Presidents, Boards of Directors and private equity funds that provided me the opportunity to solve their financial and operational issues while creating value for all. Also to Bob Rose, Ann-Ellen Hornidge, Andy Jillson and John Miller for their trust and support on many difficult projects.

My special mentors, Malcolm Minsk and Jerry Siegel, for more than forty years of friendship and professional guidance. Jerry you are missed.

The endorsements of my book have come from business professionals who I truly respect; Jerry Goldress, Alex Gregory, Ann-Ellen Hornidge, Harry Maziar, Bernie Marcus, Jess Meyers and Rafael Pastor. Thank you for taking the time to make this book special.

Stew and Bev, Alan and Jackie, Donna and Cary, Barry and Barbara, David and Susan, Ray, Scott, Gershon ben Fival, Lynn and Gary, Jeff and Fran, Danny and Rhonda and all who have listened, laughed and lived with me through life's roller coaster ride. Thanks to the Thursday night gaming committee for all the laughs and to the Bad Boy Bikers.

Index

Even if you've never been shot at or been the victim of fraud, if you have any comments or stories to share, please contact Lee@TheTurnaroundAuthority.com